Also by Stan Lee

Origins of Marvel Comics
Son of Origins of Marvel Comics

BRING ON THE BAD GUYS
ORIGINS OF MARVEL VILLAINS

STAN LEE

SIMON AND SCHUSTER
NEW YORK

Copyright © 1976 by Marvel Comics Group,
A Division of Cadence Industries Corporation
All rights reserved
including the right of reproduction
in whole or in part in any form
Published by Simon and Schuster
A Gulf + Western Company
Rockefeller Center, 630 Fifth Avenue
New York, New York 10020

Manufactured in the United States of America
  2 3 4 5 6 7 8 9 10

Library of Congress Cataloging in Publication Data

Lee, Stan.
    Bring on the bad guys.

    1. Marvel Comic Group. 2. Comic books, strips, etc.—United States. I. Title.
PN6725.L37   741.5′973   76-22779
ISBN 0-671-22354-2
ISBN 0-671-22355-0 pbk.

To you, the literate comicbook fan, this volume is gratefully dedicated.

In one brief decade, your enthusiasm, your interest, and your unwavering support have helped make an entire generation increasingly aware that the ubiquitous comic is not only a major contemporary art form, but truly an integral part of our cultural heritage.

Hey—thanks a lot!

PROLOGUE

I yield to no one in my love for heroes. Especially Marvel heroes. And yet—

I'll tell you a secret. I've always been fascinated by the villains. Sure, I know they're evil. Sure, I know they're up to no good. Sure, I know they're a threat to our wallets and our freedom and they may be injurious to our health. You needn't tell me how thoroughly rotten they are; I've spent most of my life dreaming up ways for our good guys to fight them. And yet—

You've got to admit they're colorful. You've got to admit they're interesting. You've got to admit they wear the craziest costumes, and sport the wildest way-out names. And, most of all, you've got to admit our heroes need them . . . as much as they need Blue Cross! After all, if not for the villains the good guys would either have to apply for welfare or be reduced to battling each other, and, given the normal rate of attrition, Marvel Comics might soon be out of business—a possibility too traumatically tragic to contemplate.

But seriously, folks. Once we've invented a hero, that's it. He's pretty much the same, issue after issue. He's predictable. And that's only natural, because we've had time to get to know him, to learn to anticipate his reactions. But each new story needs a new baddie for him to battle, and that's where the fun comes in. Our villain has to be unique, clever, inventive, and full of fiendish surprises. And we never get a chance to tire of him—if our hero knows his stuff, he won't be around long enough to bore us.

See what I mean? Endowed with a group of great heroes—and we wouldn't be interested in any other kind—the main appeal of our frisky little fables must lie with the villains we concoct. What new threats can they pose to our unsuspecting protagonists? What new weapons will they soon unleash upon a dazed and defenseless world? What new powers can they bring to bear that will give our good guys a run for their dough?

But they mustn't just be evil. They mustn't just be strong. They've also got to be unusual, exciting, provocative, and surprising. Now, how can you help but dig a gang like that? I always end up loving them, and, judging by our fan mail, so do you.

It's true. At least fifty percent of your madly enthusiastic epistles deal with comments and critiques concerning our multifaceted little evil-doers. That's why most of our Bullpen story conferences are concerned with the selection of the right villain for the right hero, and, most important of all, with ways of making you care about the villain. For, make no mistake about it, you've got to be as interested in the scoundrel as you are in the stalwart in order for the story to work.

One final point, and then I'll let you get on to the good stuff. You've probably noticed that we always try to motivate our miscreant as much as we do our hero. We hate to have a varlet doing evil just for the sake of being naughty. We try to indicate why he does the things he does, what made him the way he is. And, wherever possible, we may even let him exhibit some decent, likable traits. In the magic world of Marvel, not even supervillains need be all bad, just as our superheroes are rarely all good; they usually display some natural, human failings, even as you and I—granted, of course, that you and I are human.

Okay. That's it. We dare not permit ourselves the luxury of any more leisurely chitchat while our malevolent menaces are lurking amongst the pages ahead. The stage is set. The lights are dim. You and I—heroes all—are about to share some of the most momentous confrontations in all of comicdom. Only one thing yet remains—

Bring on the bad guys!

Stan Lee
New York, 1976

8

PART 1

DOCTOR DOOM ™

THE MADNESS
BEHIND THE MASK!

Sometimes you're lucky. Sometimes you hit a homer first time at bat. That's how it was with Jack and me—and Doctor Doom.

We had already produced the first four issues of *The Fantastic Four,* and we knew we had a hit. Our cosmic-powered quartet had taken the comicbook world by storm, but Jack and I knew we had to keep coming up with new ideas so the fans wouldn't feel we were just a flash in the pan. And new ideas, to us, meant just one thing. We had to find a supervillain that would totally turn on the minions of Marveldom.

But, before I continue to hold you spellbound with this colorful chronicle, let's backtrack just a bit. There's always the chance that someone might have recklessly bought this book without first having read our two previous masterworks, *Origins of Marvel Comics* and *Son of Origins.* For any such hapless soul, helplessly wondering what this is all about, I'll try to painlessly clue you in as we go zooming along.

Let's travel back in memory to the early part of 1962. It was a vintage year for Marvel Comics because we had successfully launched *The Fantastic Four,* an offbeat saga about three guys and a gal who attempted to make the first manned flight to the moon, but crashed back to Earth when their primitive little ship was brutally battered by a barrage of powerful cosmic rays. Though they survived the emergency landing, the mysterious rays had affected each of them in a different way, giving each one a strange and awesome super power. No need to describe those powers now; if you don't already know, they'll become crystal clear as soon as you reach the part with the pictures. Anyway, Jack and I had already completed the first four issues of the good ol' *F.F.*, and that brings us up to date. Ah, but somewhere in the distance I hear a muffled cry, an anguished voice, calling, asking, beseeching, "Jack who?" And I hasten to reply.

Much as I hate to admit it, I didn't produce our little Marvel masterpieces all by myself. No, mine was the task of originating the basic concept, and then writing the script—penning the darling little dialogue balloons and cuddly captions that have been such a source of inspiration to scholars and shut-ins everywhere. However, I've long been privileged to collaborate with some of the most talented artists of all, artists who would take my rough-hewn plots and refine them into the illustrated stories that have made the name of Marvel almost as famous as pastafazool. Heading the list of such artists who have helped create what has come to be known as The Marvel Age of Comics is Jolly Jack Kirby. I originally dubbed him Jolly Jack because it was impossible to tell if he was smiling or not behind the massive cigar which formed a protective smoke screen around him while he worked. However, to prevent you from worrying needlessly, I'll hasten to add that he did eventually come up for air, and later on, because of his cataclysmic creativity and countless contributions to our Marvel mythology, I hung the sobriquet of King before his last name. Thus today, readers everywhere refer to the jolly one as Jack King Kirby. But, moving right along . . .

There we were, Jack and I, pacing back and forth in the Bullpen, trying to dream up some soul-stirring, senses-staggering, super-sensational new villain to take the comicbook world by storm. Well, you know me. I'm strictly a name freak. I'm a sucker for any name with a zingy rhythm, a dramatic sound, a litanous lilt. Seeking a name that suggested lethal menace, I latched onto the word "doom". But all by itself it was just a syllable—a simple sound. It needed something more—another syllable, an additional sound, something to give it oomph.

Doom Man didn't seem to do the trick, and Mister Doom didn't quite have it. Professor Doom just left me cold, while even the alliterative Donald Doom fell a little short. But then, scant seconds before I'd be forced to resort to Doom the Dentist, I had it! Doctor Doom! Eloquent in its simplicity—magnificent in its implied menace!

But Kirby was always a tough guy to impress. I could see by the expression on his face that he was about to ask me if Doc Doom was a specialist or a general practitioner. And did he make house calls?

12

However, minutes later, after we began to swap ideas, I knew I'd reached him. Whenever something is really right, it never takes long to put it all together. Each little idea led to another, more exciting one. We'd make him far more than just the usual stereotyped mad scientist; we'd give him a mysterious past, a secret cache of unlimited wealth (which we'd explain in some future yarn—once we figured it out), a face too gruesome for the reader to behold, and an ego so great that it would match that of Reed Richards himself. In fact, we'd make him an actual contemporary of Reed's—an old schoolmate—which I thought was a terrific touch. As for the costume, and the iron mask, it seems that in those days we just couldn't do anything wrong. To this very day, ol' Victor Von Doom is probably Marvel's very top villain, in appearance, in power, personality, and plain sheer reader appeal.

The only problem with him was—as it so often happened in Marvel stories—we didn't get a chance to present his origin till long after the first Dr. Doom yarn appeared. You see, we liked him well enough when we dreamed him up, but we had no way of knowing he'd become our answer to Professor Moriarty. We had no way of knowing the readers would demand more, more, more! As far as we knew, he'd make a perfect villain for issue #5, and that was that. So we did the best we could with him, wove him into a tight little plot, drew the pictures, wrote the story, sent the whole works off to the printer, and promptly forgot about him as we began work on the next issue of *The Hulk*.

But, though we forgot about him, the hordes of Marveldom Assembled did not. Within a matter of days the mail came flying in. And it all carried the same message. Bring back Dr. Doom! Well, there were no flies on us. After the first thousand or so letters, we suspected we had a hit! So bring him back we did.

However, it wasn't till the year 1964 that we really had time to do the kind of origin tale I felt Doc Doom deserved. I wanted a saga of epic proportions, one that would make the reader really understand what motivated him, what had turned him into a villain, what made him the tragic, tortured tyrant he was. I wanted the kind of story that would have made a perfect 1940's movie, with such old time actors as Basil Rathbone, Peter Lorre, and John Carradine. And Jack caught the mood exactly. He felt just the same way. He couldn't have turned out the illustrated masterpiece he did unless he was living it with every pencil stroke. I'm especially fond of this particular origin story because it serves as a perfect example of the way I prefer to see a villain portrayed. Menacing, yes. Evil, perhaps. And yet, far too complex to be neatly labelled as a typical bad guy. I think of him, instead, as a man with his own drives, his own needs, his own pains and frustrations; a man to be feared, to be shunned, but also to be studied and—perhaps—even pitied.

Incidentally, I'd like you to notice the difference in art styles between the two Dr. Doom strips. Remember, they were drawn about two years apart, and comparing them will give you a good opportunity to see one of the things that has made Marvel grow into the world's largest comicbook company. That thing, of course, is the almost uncanny ability of our entire staff—artists, writers, letterers, colorists, everybody—to continually improve with every new strip.

You'll notice a new maturity, new depth and dramatic impact in both the script and artwork. You'll see why, by the year 1964, Marvel had already attracted the attention of a large and ever-growing college audience. And, most of all, you'll see Dr. Doom as few have ever seen him before. You'll see one of the world of fiction's most famous characters as child, youth, and finally man—a man far different than any other who ever strode this planet.

And so, the time has come to begin our incredible journey—a journey into the past, into the distant days of Marvel Comics, when a new and awesome type of villainy was just aborning. We'll begin with the very first appearance of Dr. Doom, as readers everywhere initially met him, in the momentous fifth issue of *The Fantastic Four*, in the story entitled "Prisoners of Dr. Doom"....

THE FANTASTIC FOUR,™ IN...
"PRISONERS OF DOCTOR DOOM!"

MILES AWAY, IN THE HEART OF NEW YORK, A TOWERING SKYSCRAPER BECOMES EMPTY AS ITS OCCUPANTS LEAVE FOR HOME AT THE END OF A TYPICAL WORK DAY...

ONE BY ONE THE BUILDING'S LIGHTS FLICKER OUT...

...ALL EXCEPT THOSE AT THE TOWER! THE TOWER WHICH SERVES AS HEADQUARTERS OF *THE FANTASTIC FOUR!*

AND, WITHIN THE TOWER WE FIND...

WHAT ARE YOU READING, JOHNNY?

A GREAT NEW COMIC MAG, REED! *SAY!* YOU KNOW SOMETHING--!

I'LL BE DOGGONED IF THIS MONSTER DOESN'T REMIND ME OF *THE THING!*

VER-RY FUNNY!

GIMME THAT MAG, SQUIRT! I'LL TEACH YA TO COMPARE ME TO A COMIC BOOK MONSTER!

HEY!

IF YOU WANT IT SO BAD, I'LL *WARM IT UP* FOR YOU, BIG MAN!

OWW!

COME *BACK* HERE!

COME 'N *GET* ME!

2

16

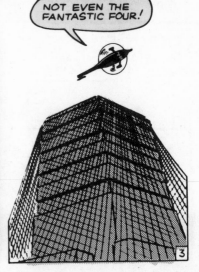

LOOK! SOME SORT OF *NET* HAS BEEN DROPPED OVER THE ENTIRE TOWER!

BURN *THRU* IT, HOT SHOT!

I'M *TRYING* TO, THING, BUT IT MUST BE ASBESTOS!

FANTASTIC FOUR!! HEED MY WORDS! THIS IS DOCTOR DOOM!!

DOCTOR DOOM!? WHO--? WHAT IS HE?

THAT VOICE! I *RECOGNIZE* IT! BUT-- I THOUGHT HE WAS *DEAD!*

YEARS AGO, IN MY COLLEGE DAYS, THERE WAS A STUDENT NAMED VICTOR VON DOOM, WHO WAS FASCINATED BY SORCERY AND BLACK MAGIC!

I, VON DOOM, HAVE MASTERED THE MYSTIC RITES!

HE WAS A BRILLIANT SCIENCE STUDENT, BUT HE WAS ONLY INTERESTED IN FORBIDDEN EXPERIMENTS!

THIS IS *MAD,* VON DOOM! WHY DO YOU KEEP TRYING TO CONTACT THE NETHER WORLD?

SILENCE! JUST DO AS YOU ARE TOLD!

ONE NIGHT, THE EVIL GENIUS WENT TOO FAR, AS HE BROUGHT FORTH POWERS WHICH EVEN *HE* COULD NOT CONTROL!

WHAT *WAS* THAT?

IT CAME FROM VON DOOM'S DORMITORY!

HE MANAGED TO ESCAPE WITH HIS LIFE, ALTHOUGH HIS FACE WAS BADLY DISFIGURED! AND THEN...

VON DOOM, I AM *EXPELLING* YOU FROM THIS SCHOOL BEFORE YOU CAUSE GREATER HARM TO YOUR-SELF, OR TO US!

AND SO HE LEFT! WHEN LAST HEARD OF, HE WAS PROWLING THE WASTELANDS OF TIBET, STILL SEEKING FORBIDDEN SECRETS OF BLACK MAGIC AND SORCERY!

AND NOW, THE SINISTER GENIUS IS HOVERING ABOVE US!

THIS WELL COULD BE THE PRELUDE TO THE MOST DANGEROUS ADVENTURE OF OUR CAREER!

4

YOU ARE MY **PRISONERS**, ALL OF YOU! IF YOU WISH ME TO SPARE YOUR LIVES, DO **EXACTLY** AS I COMMAND!

FIRST, SEND SUSAN STORM OUT TO ME! I SHALL HOLD HER AS A **HOSTAGE** TO INSURE THAT YOU DO WHAT I DEMAND OF YOU! NOW WHAT IS YOUR ANSWER?

I'LL GIVE HIM HIS ANSWER! FIRST, I'LL SNAP THIS PUNY NET JUST THE WAY I'LL SNAP HIS RIBS WHEN I GET A HOLD OF HIM! AND THEN...

YEOWW!

LET GO, THING! IT'S ELECTRICALLY CHARGED!

LISTEN, DOOM, OR GOON, OR WHATEVER YOU CALL YOURSELF! YOU AIN'T GETTIN' SUE IN THAT CORNY-LOOKIN' PLANE OF YOURS NO MATTER **WHAT**! IF YOU **WANT** US, YOU COME HERE AND TRY 'N **GET** US!

EASY, THING! DON'T LOSE YOUR TEMPER! IT'S STILL **HIS** MOVE!

I-I'VE **GOT** TO GO OUT TO HIM! IT'S THE ONLY WAY TO BRING HIM OUT INTO THE OPEN! IF HE'S AS DANGEROUS AS YOU SAY, WE **CAN'T** JUST SCARE HIM OFF! WE'VE GOT TO **FIGHT** HIM!

YOU'RE **RIGHT**, SUE! THERE MAY BE **MORE** THAN THE FOUR OF US AT STAKE! BUT I SWEAR ...HE WILL NOT HARM YOU -- NOT WHILE WE LIVE!!

IF YOU ARE SENDING HER OUT, SHOOT UP A FLARE, AND I SHALL OPEN A SECTION OF THE NET FOR HER! AH, THE FLARE! **GOOD! GOOD!**

DOCTOR DOOM MUST HAVE **VAST POWERS** TO DARE CHALLENGE THE FANTASTIC FOUR!! AND THIS IS THE ONLY WAY TO FIND OUT WHAT THOSE POWERS **ARE**!

I AM READY, DOCTOR DOOM! I WILL BE YOUR HOSTAGE!

BUT YOU SHALL LIVE TO **REGRET** DEFYING THE FANTASTIC FOUR!!

5

19

AH! THEY AGREE TO BOARD MY SHIP, AS I *PLANNED* THEY WOULD! I *KNEW* MISTER FANTASTIC COULD NOT RESIST TRYING TO LEARN WHAT MY MISSION IS!

ONE FLIP OF A SWITCH AND THEY WILL BE *MINE!*

HOLY SMOKE, REED! THIS DOCTOR DOOM CHARACTER MUST BE A REAL *WIZARD* AT INVENTING THINGS!

I *TOLD* YOU HE IS AN EVIL GENIUS! WE MUST NEVER UNDERESTIMATE HIM!

SO FAR MY PLAN IS WORKING WITHOUT A HITCH!

THEN, WITH A SUDDEN, UNEXPECTED SURGE OF ROCKET POWER THE HELICOPTER BLAZES THRU THE SKY AT ALMOST UNBELIEVABLE SPEED!

WE WILL REACH MY CASTLE STRONGHOLD WITHIN MINUTES!

AND NOW, MY RELUCTANT PASSENGERS, WELCOME TO THE HOME OF DOCTOR DOOM!

IT--IT'S A REGULAR *FORTRESS!*

7

MINUTES LATER...

WELL, WHAT ARE WE *WAITIN'* FOR? LET'S *RUSH* 'IM!

WE *CAN'T*, THING! WE PROMISED NOT TO ATTACK HIM TILL WE HEAR HIM OUT!

YOU ARE WISE TO RESTRAIN YOURSELVES! FAST THOUGH YOU MAY BE, MY LITTLE PET HERE IS *FASTER!*

NOW THAT WE ARE ALL TOGETHER, I HAVE A MISSION FOR YOU TO PERFORM FOR ME! IF YOU CARRY IT OUT SUCCESSFULLY, YOU WILL ALL BE REWARDED! IF NOT, I HAVE A HOSTAGE!

TALK FAST, MISTER! WHAT *IS* THE MISSION?

I HAVE SUCCESSFULLY DEVELOPED THE MOST INCREDIBLE INVENTION OF THE AGE... AN ACTUAL *TIME TRAVEL DEVICE!* AND I WANT YOU TO GO CENTURIES INTO THE PAST AND OBTAIN THE LEGENDARY TREASURE OF *BLACKBEARD* FOR ME!

HE--HE *MEANS* IT!!

WHY DON'T YOU GO GET THAT TREASURE *YOURSELF?*

I *CANNOT!* I MUST REMAIN HERE TO OPERATE THE MACHINE!

WELL, SHALL WE *DO* IT?

GOSH! A CHANCE TO ACTUALLY VISIT THE *PAST!* WHO COULD *REFUSE?*

I *COULD!* WHAT IF HE DOESN'T BRING US *BACK?*

I WANT THAT TREASURE! I SHALL BRING YOU BACK!

DESPITE HIS OTHER FAULTS, DOOM IS NOT A LIAR! HE WILL KEEP HIS WORD!

HE'D *BETTER!*

DOOM, IF WE *DON'T* RETURN... SWEAR YOU WILL SET SUE FREE!

DONE! I ONLY NEEDED HER TO LURE YOU HERE!

AND NOW, I SHALL SEND YOU BACK... HUNDREDS OF YEARS INTO THE PAST! YOU WILL HAVE FORTY-EIGHT HOURS TO BRING ME BLACKBEARD'S TREASURE CHEST! *DO NOT FAIL!*

LOOK! WHAT'S THAT BUTTON HE'S PRESSING?

8

24

PART 3

"ON THE TRAIL OF BLACKBEARD"

HOURS LATER, THE THING IS FIRST TO AWAKEN...

...SLOWLY, SILENTLY, HE LOOKS ABOUT HIM...

...ONLY TO FIND THAT THEY ARE LOCKED IN THE MUSTY HOLD OF A PIRATE SHIP!

YOU TWO CAN GO BACK IF YOU WANNA! AS FOR ME, I LIKE IT HERE!

REED! HE ACTUALLY ENJOYS BEING BLACKBEARD!

BUT HE CAN'T REMAIN HERE IN THE PAST!

WHY CAN'T I STAY? THE FUTURE HOLDS NOTHING FOR ME! IN THE TWENTIETH CENTURY I'M NOTHIN' BUT A MONSTER... A FREAK!

BUT HERE I'M SOMEBODY! I'M A LEADER OF MEN! I'M A CAPTAIN! I'M THE GUY WHO STARTED THE LEGEND OF BLACKBEARD! THE KIDS WILL READ ABOUT ME IN SCHOOL SOME DAY! I AIN'T GIVIN' THIS UP ...NEVER!

AND I'LL MAKE SURE YOU TWO DON'T TRY TO TAKE ME BACK! TIE 'EM UP, MEN-- FAST!

DON'T BE SCARED OF THE TORCH! HE'S STILL SOAKIN' WET! HE CAN'T FLAME ON YET!

THAT'S IT! WRAP A SAIL AROUND MR. FANTASTIC! IT WON'T DO HIM ANY GOOD TO STRETCH IF HE'S GOT NO PLACE TO STRETCH OUT OF!

NOW PUT 'EM OVER THE SIDE IN A LIFE BOAT! BY THE TIME THEY GET FREE, WE'LL HAVE LOST OURSELVES IN THE FOG!! THEY'LL NEVER FIND US AGAIN!

THING! DON'T DO IT!! DON'T CUT YOURSELF OFF FROM US! YOU MUSTN'T! YOU'LL REGRET IT SOME DAY!! DON'T DO IT!!

AT THAT VERY MOMENT, AS THOUGH IN ECHO TO THE TORCH'S WORDS...

AHOY, ALL HANDS!! TWISTER AHEAD!

17

THE GALE IS *FREEING* ME!! I CAN *MOVE* AGAIN! TORCH! WHERE ARE YOU??

OVER *HERE*, REED!! WE--WE'RE BEING WASHED OVERBOARD!! *REED!!* HELP!!

SECONDS LATER, AS SUDDENLY AS IT HAD APPEARED, THE FURY OF THE STORM BLOWS ITSELF OUT TO SEA...

REED!! THING!! HELP!!

EASY, LAD! I SEE YOU! *HANG ON!*

C-CAN'T STAY AFLOAT MUCH LONGER...

GOSH, REED... I-- I WAS ALMOST DONE FOR!

YOU'RE ALRIGHT NOW, TORCH! BUT WE'VE GOT TO FIND THE THING! IT'S ALMOST TIME FOR DOCTOR DOOM TO BRING US BACK!

THERE HE IS...WASHED ASHORE!

HIS DISGUISE MUST HAVE BEEN BLOWN OFF BY THE STORM!

DON'T *SAY* IT, RUBBER MAN! I *KNOW!* I WAS A FOOL! I MUSTA GOT CARRIED AWAY BY BEING ACCEPTED--AS A NORMAL MAN-- EVEN IF IT WAS ONLY BY A BAND OF CUT-THROAT PIRATES! I--I JUST LOST MY DUMB HEAD FOR AWHILE!

WE'RE IN LUCK, REED! HERE'S THE PIRATE CHEST! IT WAS WASHED ASHORE, ALSO!

BUT NOW, HOW IS DOCTOR DOOM GONNA GET US BACK TO THE PRESENT?

AT THAT INSTANT, ACROSS THE GULF OF CENTURIES, A HAND ACTIVATES AN ATOMIC POWER CIRCUIT, AND...

THEY HAVE HAD ENOUGH TIME TO OBTAIN THE GEMS OF BLACKBEARD FOR ME! AND IF THEY FAILED, THEY WILL DIE!

18

WE PROMISED TO BRING YOU BLACKBEARD'S TREASURE CHEST, DOOM! WELL, HERE IT *IS!*

GOOD! GOOD! THE GEMS IN THAT CHEST WILL HELP ME GAIN MASTERY OF ALL THE WORLD!

THOSE LITTLE BAUBLES ARE *MORE* THAN WHAT THEY SEEM! THEY WERE ORIGINALLY THE PROPERTY OF *MERLIN,* THE ANCIENT MAGICIAN! HE GAVE THEM MYSTIC POWER...THE POWER TO MAKE THEIR OWNER *INVINCIBLE!*

AND NOW, THAT POWER SHALL BE *MINE!* WITH THESE GEMS IN MY POSSESSION, NO FORCE ON EARTH CAN EVER DEFEAT ME!

REED! THE GEMS WERE SCATTERED TO THE BOTTOM OF THE SEA DURING THE STORM!! WHAT IF *SUB-MARINER** SHOULD EVER FIND THEM??!

WE'LL JUST HAVE TO PRAY THAT HE NEVER DOES, TORCH!

WHA--??! *CHAINS!!* WORTHLESS CHAINS!! I'VE BEEN *TRICKED!*

YOU'RE GONNA BE MORE THAN THAT, BROTHER! LET'S *GET* 'IM, GUYS!

FOOL!! YOU THINK YOU CAN DEFEAT DOCTOR DOOM SO EASILY??!

YEAH!! JUST *WATCH* ME!

HEY!!!?

IT'S NOTHIN' BUT A *ROBOT!*

NATURALLY! I AM IN A HIDDEN ROOM ABOVE YOU! A ROOM FROM WHICH I SHALL NOW PRESS A BUTTON DRAINING YOUR CHAMBER OF ALL OXYGEN! *FAREWELL,* FANTASTIC FOUR!

* "SUB-MARINER"... SEE FANTASTIC FOUR, ISSUE #4, MAY

TOO BAD YOU CANNOT FLAME ON, TORCH, BUT WITHOUT OXYGEN, FIRE WILL NOT BURN! *NONE* CAN BETRAY DOCTOR DOOM!

HE'S FORGOTTEN ABOUT *ME!* THERE'S STILL ONE CHANCE...

BY BECOMING INVISIBLE, I CAN EDGE UP TO HIS CONTROL PANEL! NOW, IF I CAN JUST ACTIVATE HIS CUT-OFF SWITCH, TO SHORT-CIRCUIT THE MECHANISM!

I *DID* IT!

IT OPENED THE ESCAPE DOOR! NOW, IF I CAN JUST REACH THE OTHERS IN TIME!

AIR... GOT TO HAVE AIR...

HANG ON... SAVE YOUR BREATH... HANG ON!

-GASP- MAYBE I CAN BREAK UP THE FLOOR.!!...MAYBE THERE'S AIR UNDER- NEATH...

AND, JUST OUTSIDE THE AIR-TIGHT CHAMBER...

IF ONLY I'M NOT TOO LATE!

AIR!! AT LAST! WE'RE *SAVED!*

THING! TORCH! *LOOK!* IT'S... *SUE!*

I PRAYED I'D FIND THAT HIDDEN DOOR RELEASE BUTTON IN TIME!

THANK HEAVEN YOU'RE UNHARMED, SUE!

BUT WHAT DO WE DO *NOW?*

21

NOW, I'LL JUST CREATE A CIRCLE OF FLAME AROUND THE CASTLE, AND SMOKE DOCTOR DOOM OUT!!

BAH! LET HIM USE HIS FLAME! I HOPE HE BURNS MY FORTRESS TO THE GROUND, SO THAT NONE WILL EVER LEARN MY MANY SECRETS!

AS FOR ME, THE GREATEST SCIENTIFIC BRAIN OF ALL TIME IS NOT WITHOUT HIS OWN EMERGENCY ESCAPE DEVICES...SUCH AS MY ROCKET-POWERED FLYING HARNESS!

I HAVE BEEN CHEATED OUT OF THE MAGIC GEMS OF MERLIN, BUT I SHALL STILL ESCAPE...TO FIND A NEW HIDDEN SITE WHERE I CAN PLAN FOR MY CONQUEST OF EARTH!

I'VE GOT TO GO AFTER HIM! MANKIND WILL NEVER BE SAFE IF DOCTOR DOOM ESCAPES!

EVEN YOUR MIRACULOUS FLAME CANNOT MATCH THE THRUST OF MY ROCKETS, TORCH!

HE'S RIGHT! I--I'M GROWING WEAK!

TOO MUCH STRAIN... CAN'T GO ON--FLAME DYING--

TORCH! LOOK!

GOT TO KEEP ENOUGH FLAME TO BREAK MY FALL...GOT TO...

TORCH!! THAT WAS A GREAT TRY!

BAH! THEY DON'T PAY OFF FOR ALSO-RANS!

GOSH, FIRST SUB-MARINER, AND NOW DOCTOR DOOM LOOSE ON EARTH! WHAT HAPPENS NEXT?!

WE'LL DEVOTE OUR LIVES TO TRACKING THEM DOWN! WE CAN DO NO MORE!

AND NEXT TIME I'LL HANDLE THINGS MY WAY!

the END

SURPRISE FOLLOWS SURPRISE IN THE NEXT FABULOUS ISSUE OF THE FANTASTIC FOUR!!

23

And now it's time to leap two years ahead, to the big 1964 Annual Edition of *The Fantastic Four*. This is the issue in which Dr. Doom's origin finally appeared.

One of the reasons it took a couple of years for us to whip up a satisfactory origin tale was that I really wanted this one to be something special. I wanted to explain how Victor Von Doom was able to afford his weapons, gadgets, and assorted atomic devices. Also, I wanted to go back to his childhood and establish a solid motivation for everything that followed in his adult years. But, most of all, I wanted to make him the first supervillain in comics who would actually be a king in his own country—and who would play it to the hilt.

I wish we had room to show you future stories featuring the Lord of Latveria, stories in which he can't be arrested in the United States because of his diplomatic immunity, or where Interpol is helpless to act against him because his only real crime is trying to take over the world—and that's not listed as a punishable offense! Yep, we really had some great times with Doctor Doom, and I guess he easily qualifies as my all-time favorite villain—but maybe I'm prejudiced. You see, just for a gag, Jack once drew a sketch of Doom without his mask—and guess whose face was smilin' out at you beneath the dark green hood!

"YOU ARE RIGHT, BORIS... IT IS ON A NIGHT SUCH AS THIS THAT *SHE* WOULD WANT ME TO VISIT HER!"

SLOWLY, MAJESTICALLY, THE STRANGE, BROODING, ARMOR-CLAD FIGURE FOLLOWS THE MAN WITH THE LANTERN THROUGH THE WINDING CORRIDORS OF THE WORLD'S MOST MYSTERIOUS CASTLE! NOT A SOUND IS HEARD, SAVE THE DULL TAPPING OF A HEAVY CANE, AND THE MUFFLED CLANG OF IRON BOOTS!

FOR THIS IS THE KINGDOM OF DOCTOR DOOM! KNOWN TO THE OUTSIDE-WORLD SIMPLY AS LATVERIA, IT NESTLES, VIRTUALLY UNNOTICED, IN THE HEART OF THE BAVARIAN ALPS!

AND HERE ON A LONELY, WINDSWEPT MOOR, THE TWO MEN STOP! FOR LONG MOMENTS THEY STAND, LOOKING DOWN AT AN ALMOST CONCEALED TOMBSTONE, AS THE FURY OF THE STORM LASHES THE BARREN COUNTRYSIDE! THEN, FINALLY, A DEEP VOICE BREAKS THE SILENCE!

THIS IS THE PLACE! IT WAS *HERE* THAT IT ALL BEGAN!

AND THEN, THE YEARS SEEM TO FLASH BACK, AS THE TALL, STILL FIGURE RETURNS IN MEMORY TO THE DIM, FADED PAST...

A GYPSY TRIBE HAD ONCE CAMPED ON THE VERY SPOT WHERE DOCTOR DOOM NOW STANDS! AND, THE MAN IN THE IRON MASK HAS GOOD REASON TO REMEMBER THAT DAY... FOR HE HAD BEEN ONE OF THEM!

SOMEONE FIND LITTLE VICTOR VON DOOM! THE BARON'S SOLDIERS HAVE COME TO SEIZE HIS FATHER!!

2.

AND, IN THE SIMPLE TENT OF WERNER VON DOOM...

I HAVE DONE NOTHING! I AM ONLY A GYPSY *HEALER!* I TREAT THE SICK AND SUFFERING OF MY *TRIBE!*

SILENCE! YOU ARE TO COME WITH ME! BY ORDER OF THE BARON!

DO NOT WORRY, VICTOR, MY SON! I HAVE DONE NO WRONG! I SHALL NOT BE HARMED!

THE TRIBE *NEEDS* YOU, FATHER! *I* NEED YOU!

DO NOT FEAR, VON DOOM! I SHALL LOOK AFTER THE BOY UNTIL YOU RETURN!

WHY ARE THEY *TAKING* HIM, BORIS?? HE HAS DONE NOTHING! HIS LIFE HAS BEEN SPENT IN HEALING... IN HELPING THE WEAK AND HELPLESS!

BUT HE IS A *GYPSY,* BOY... AS WE *ALL* ARE! IT IS THE PRICE WE MUST *PAY!*

THEN, TAKEN TO THE LOCAL CASTLE, WERNER VON DOOM IS BROUGHT TO THE BEDSIDE OF THE BARON'S DYING WIFE...

IT IS HOPELESS! IT IS BEYOND MY POWER TO SAVE HER!

YOU *LIE,* GYPSY! USE YOUR MAGIC POTIONS! SAVE HER... OR YOU'LL PAY WITH YOUR *OWN* WORTHLESS LIFE!!

AND SO, ALTHOUGH HE *KNOWS* IT'S FUTILE, THE GYPSY HEALER DOES WHAT HE CAN! AND, THEN...

THERE IS NOTHING MORE I CAN DO, EXCELLENCY!

THEN *GO!* BACK TO YOUR WRETCHED CAMP! AND PRAY... FOR *YOUR* SAKE... THAT YOU HAVE BEEN SUCCESSFUL!

THE BARONESS CANNOT SURVIVE TILL MORNING! *NOTHING* COULD HAVE SAVED HER! I MUST TAKE MY SON AND *FLEE...* WHILE THERE IS YET TIME!

A SHORT TIME LATER, AS THE GYPSY HAD PREDICTED...

SHE'S *DEAD!*

THE GYPSY *FAILED* ME!! BUT, HE'LL *PAY* FOR IT!... WITH HIS *OWN LIFE!*

WITHIN THE HOUR, THE BARON'S PICKED TROOPS ATTACK THE DEFENSELESS LITTLE GYPSY CAMP IN A FRANTIC ATTEMPT TO LOCATE THE MISSING GYPSY HEALER AND HIS SON...

WE'LL *FIND* HIM! THERE IS NO PLACE IN THIS KINGDOM WHERE A FUGITIVE CAN HIDE FROM THE BARON'S VENGEANCE!

HE IS NOT HERE! WE MUST COMB THE COUNTRYSIDE!

MEANWHILE... WHY DO WE RUN LIKE THIS, FATHER?? WHY DO WE NOT STAY BEHIND AND *FIGHT!*?

AHH, VICTOR... YOU SOUND LIKE YOUR DEAD MOTHER! SHE *TOO* FEARED NOTHING, NO MATTER HOW HOPELESS THE ODDS!

SUDDENLY, THE GYPSY'S HORSE BOLTS, AND...

FATE HAS DEALT US A TRAGIC BLOW! WITHOUT A HORSE, WE ARE AS GOOD AS CAPTURED!

BUT, WE SHALL *NOT* SURRENDER! NO MATTER WHAT HAPPENS TO ME, THEY WILL NEVER GET *YOU*, MY SON! FOR YOU HAVE A *DESTINY* TO FULFILL!

FATHER... I'M HUNGRY... AND COLD..!

WRAPPING HIS OWN THREADBARE GARMENTS AROUND THE SHIVERING BOY, THE DESPERATE GYPSY PLODS ON THROUGH THE NIGHT, MIRACULOUSLY EVADING HIS PURSUERS...

UNTIL, FINALLY...

VON DOOM! IT'S *ME*... BORIS!! THE SOLDIERS HAVE GONE! VON DOOM...!

THEY ARE NEARLY FROZEN! VON DOOM IS DYING... BUT THE BOY STILL HAS A CHANCE! I MUST GET THEM BACK TO CAMP!

4.

AND SO... HEED MY LAST WORDS...YOU MUST PROTECT... PROTECT... OHHH...

FATHER! NONE WILL HAVE TO PROTECT *ME*! I SHALL BECOME POWERFUL... *STRONG*! I SHALL *AVENGE* YOUR DEATH!!

HE DID NOT MEAN PROTECT THE *BOY*! HE MEANT THAT THE *WORLD* MUST BE PROTECTED... FROM THE SON WHO BEARS THE NAME *VON DOOM*!!

THEY MURDERED MY MOTHER...WHEN I WAS BUT AN INFANT!! AND NOW THEY HAVE SLAIN MY FATHER!! THEY'LL *PAY* FOR THAT!! ALL OF *MANKIND* SHALL PAY!!

WE NEVER TOLD HIM THAT HIS MOTHER WAS A MYSTIC *SORCERESS*!! AND HER BLOOD RUNS IN HIS OWN VEINS! I PRAY HE NEVER LEARNS OF HIS *DARK HERITAGE*!

BUT, AFTER THE OTHERS HAVE GONE...

THESE ARE YOUR FATHER'S HERBS AND REMEDIES! REMEMBER, LAD... HE USED THEM ONLY FOR *GOOD*!

AND MEN REPAID HIS KINDNESS BY *HOUNDING* HIM... *SLAYING* HIM!!

THEN, AFTER FAITHFUL BORIS DEPARTS ...

WHAT HAVE I *FOUND*...HIDDEN HERE BENEATH THESE HEIRLOOMS! A STRANGE *CHEST*!

THAT *NAME*! CAN IT *BE*? IT BELONGED TO...MY *MOTHER*!

MAGIC POTIONS!! STRANGE SCIENTIFIC SECRETS! WHY DID I NEVER SUSPECT?? MY MOTHER WAS A *WITCH*!

AND NOW *I* CAN LEARN HER SECRETS!!

AND SO, THE YEARS PASS...AS THIS TORMENTED BOY... THIS BRILLIANT SON OF A GENTLE, KINDLY FATHER AND A MYSTERIOUS, ENCHANTED MOTHER GROWS TO MAN-HOOD...WITH THE FEATURES OF A DEMI-GOD AND THE CUNNING OF A DEMON!

INCREDIBLE! I HAVE NEVER PLAYED BEFORE! AND YET, WHEN I TOUCH THIS FIDDLE...

IT CAN BE *YOURS*, MY LORD...FOR A *PRICE*!

BUT, VICTOR, WHY WOULD HE PAY A SMALL FORTUNE FOR A WORTH-LESS FIDDLE?

IT IS *WORTH* IT, BORIS, BECAUSE OF THIS LITTLE DEVICE! FOR, *THIS* IS WHAT CAUSES THE FIDDLE TO PLAY!

5.

AND NOW THAT WE ARE SAFELY ON OUR WAY, I'LL SHUT IT *OFF*!

WHAT KIND OF SCIENTIFIC SORCERY IS THAT ?!!

BAH! IT IS A CHILDISH TRICK... NOT WORTHY OF MY *GREAT TALENTS!*

BZZZ!

AND, A FEW MILES AWAY... BACK IN TOWN...

WHAT HAS *HAPPENED* ?!! THE FIDDLE NO LONGER *PLAYS*!!

SCRATCH!

SCRATCH!

SCRATCH!

IT WAS THAT YOUNG GYPSY... WITH THE EVIL EYE !! HE *TRICKED* ME ! BUT HE'LL *PAY* FOR IT !!

MORE AND MORE INCIDENTS OCCUR... INCIDENTS INVOLVING A HANDSOME, GLIB-TONGUED YOUNG GYPSY AND HIS SEEMINGLY MAGICAL WARES...

OTTO! I HEARD YOU CRY OUT !! WHAT... ??

LOOK! LOOK AT MY *HEAD!* THAT GYPSY'S SALVE CURED MY HEADACHE... BUT LOOK WHAT HAPPENED TO MY *HAIR!*

CALL OUT THE *GUARDS!!* SOMEONE HAS STOLEN THE *GOLD STATUE* I BOUGHT FROM THAT YOUNG GYPSY !!

NO, EXCELLENCY ! IT HAS *NOT* BEEN STOLEN !! AS SOON AS HE LEFT, I SAW IT *CHANGE* !! IT TURNED INTO THAT LUMP OF *MUD* YOU SEE BEFORE YOU !

FINALLY, THE ENTIRE COUNTRYSIDE IS UP IN ARMS !! THEN, AFTER WEEKS OF INTENSIVE SEARCHING, THE BRILLIANT YOUNG GYPSY IS CAPTURED AND SENTENCED TO A SWIFT EXECUTION BEFORE A FIRING SQUAD!

FIRE!!

YOU SHALL ALL LIVE TO REGRET THIS !!

HOW CAN HE STAND THERE AND SPEAK AFTER OUR BULLETS HAVE STRUCK HIM ?!!

AND THERE, ON THAT DATE, IN A REMOTE BALKAN KINGDOM, THE WORLD FIRST LEARNED OF VICTOR VON DOOM'S GENIUS FOR MAKING LIFE-LIKE *ROBOTS* !!

WE DID NOT CAPTURE THE GYPSY *AFTER ALL* ! IT IS SOME KIND OF *MECHANICAL MAN* !!

6.

AS TIME WENT BY, THE ELUSIVE YOUNG GYPSY BECAME A LEGEND! HE KEPT NONE OF HIS WEALTH, BUT GAVE IT TO THE POOR! NO MAN COULD GUESS WHAT HIS REAL MOTIVES WERE... AND NO MAN, OR GROUP OF MEN, COULD *CATCH* HIM!

HE'S IN THAT GYPSY CARAVAN! *FIRE!!*

IMPOSSIBLE! OUR SHELL BOUNCES OFF THE WAGON LIKE A PIECE OF *RUBBER!*

THEY DIDN'T KNOW THAT I *TREATED* EACH WAGON WITH SOME OF MY OWN SPECIAL COMPOUNDS... MAKING THEM IMPERVIOUS TO ANY TYPE OF SHELL!!

BUT NOW, LET US SEE HOW IMPERVIOUS *THEY* ARE TO MY LATEST WEAPON... A QUICK-ACTING *FREEZE-GRENADE!!*

DOES THE GYPSY FOOL THINK HE CAN STOP THIS MIGHTY TANK WITH A MERE *GRENADE??* KEEP ADVANCING, AND... *WHA...??!*

IT IS NOT AN *ORDINARY* WEAPON!! THAT IS NO NORMAL EXPLOSION... THE TEMPERATURE HAS SUDDENLY DROPPED *ONE HUNDRED DEGREES!*

RUN...RUN!! THE TANK HAS COMPLETELY *FROZEN!!*

IT'S TURNED INTO A GIANT CAKE OF *ICE!*

FLEE!! WE MAY BE *NEXT!!*

AND SO THE LEGEND OF THE STRANGE YOUNG GYPSY CONTINUED TO GROW, JUST AS HIS *POWER* GREW! SOON, NO MAN DARED DEFY THIS GIFTED, GRIM YOUNG MAN! AND THEN, ONE DAY...

MASTER! A STRANGER HAS ARRIVED... TO SEE YOU!

A *STRANGER!?*

YOU ARE NOT OF THIS COUNTRY?

THAT'S RIGHT! I'M AN *AMERICAN!* I'M DEAN OF SCIENCE AT STATE UNIVERSITY! I'VE HEARD SOME VERY INTERESTING THINGS ABOUT YOU, VON DOOM!

7.

IT'S TAKEN ME *MONTHS* TO FIND YOU! BUT AFTER SEEING SOME OF YOUR INVENTIONS, IT WAS WELL *WORTH* IT!

I'M PREPARED TO OFFER YOU A *SCHOLARSHIP* AT MY UNIVERSITY!

THAT WOULD ALLOW ME TO HAVE THE LATEST SCIENTIFIC APPARATUS AT MY DISPOSAL! HMMM....

YOU REMAIN HERE, BORIS, WITH THE OTHERS! I SHALL RETURN ONE DAY, TO REWARD YOU FOR YOUR LOYALTY!

AS YOU WISH, MASTER! NOTHING SHALL CHANGE UNTIL YOU COME BACK TO US!!

BEFORE THE DAY HAD ENDED, VICTOR VON DOOM WAS ABOARD A PLANE, HEADING FOR A NEW WORLD, AND A NEW DESTINY!

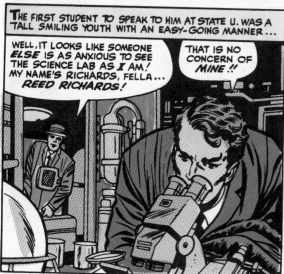

THE FIRST STUDENT TO SPEAK TO HIM AT STATE U. WAS A TALL SMILING YOUTH WITH AN EASY-GOING MANNER...

WELL, IT LOOKS LIKE SOMEONE *ELSE* IS AS ANXIOUS TO SEE THE SCIENCE LAB AS *I* AM! MY NAME'S RICHARDS, FELLA... *REED RICHARDS!*

THAT IS NO CONCERN OF *MINE!!*

LOOK, I DON'T KNOW WHY YOU'VE GOT THAT KING-SIZED CHIP ON YOUR SHOULDER, BUT BEING WE'RE *BOTH* HERE ON SCIENCE SCHOLARSHIPS, HOW ABOUT US *ROOMING* TOGETHER!?

I HAVE NO WISH TO SHARE A ROOM WITH *ANYONE!* I DESIRE *PRIVACY!!*

WELL, IT'S NONE OF MY BUSINESS, BUT AREN'T YOU CARRYING THIS "MAD SCIENTIST" BIT A LITTLE TOO FAR?

MEN ALWAYS THINK THAT THEIR SUPERIORS ARE MAD!

I HAVE SAID *ENOUGH!* NOW I SHALL FIND MY OWN QUARTERS!

I'M GLAD HE *DIDN'T* ACCEPT MY OFFER! THERE'S SOMETHING *OMINOUS* ABOUT HIM... I CAN *SENSE* IT!!

8.

SAY, PAL...ISN'T THAT REED RICHARDS IN THERE? I HEARD HE'S THE BIGGEST BRAIN ON THE CAMPUS!

I AM NOT YOUR "PAL"! AS FOR THE IDENTITY OF THAT NAÏVE, PRYING SIMPLETON...I COULD NOT CARE LESS!

YOU'VE GOT YOURSELF A NEW ROOMIE, RICHARDS! THE NAME'S BEN GRIMM! I FIGURE I'LL BE MORE LAUGHS THAN THE NUT WHO JUST FLEW OUTTA HERE!

BEN GRIMM, THE TOUCHDOWN KING? GLAD TO HAVE YOU, BIG FELLA!

IN THE DAYS THAT FOLLOWED, VICTOR VON DOOM DID SUCCEED IN FINALLY GETTING A SMALL ROOM FOR HIMSELF...A ROOM IN WHICH HE CARRIED ON BIZARRE AND DANGEROUS EXPERIMENTS!

MY KNOWLEDGE...MY POWER...THEY INCREASE WITH EACH PASSING DAY...

AND, ONE LAZY AFTERNOON, VON DOOM HAD A CALLER...

I WONDER HOW HAPPY BOY IS MAKING OUT!?

HELLO! ANYBODY HOME??

WOW! HE'S BEEN EXPERIMENTING WITH MATTER TRANSMUTATION AND DIMENSION WARPS! THIS IS PRETTY FAR-OUT STUFF!

OH...THERE YOU ARE! LISTEN, FELLA...YOU'D BETTER DOUBLE-CHECK SOME OF THESE EQUATIONS! YOU'RE OFF A FEW DECIMALS IN SOME PLACES, AND THAT COULD MEAN...

GIVE ME THAT! NOW GET OUT! DID YOU HEAR ME?? GET OUT!!

IF HE EVER COMES SNOOPING AGAIN, HE'LL LIVE TO REGRET IT!!

I FIXED UP YOUR GADGET THE WAY YOU TOLD ME TO! BUT I STILL DON'T LIKE IT, VON DOOM!

9.

IF THE FACULTY STAFF EVER LEARNS THAT YOU'VE BEEN CONDUCTING FORBIDDEN EXPERIMENTS... TRYING TO CONTACT THE NETHER WORLD...

SILENCE! JUST DO AS YOU'RE TOLD! THROW THE SWITCH!

BUT THE GYPSY GENIUS HAD MADE THE MISTAKE OF UNDERESTIMATING REED RICHARDS! FOR REED HAD BEEN RIGHT! VON DOOM'S EQUATIONS WERE A FEW DECIMALS OFF, AND SO...

WHAT WAS THAT?

IT CAME FROM VON DOOM'S DORMITORY ROOM!

HIS HELPER MIRACULOUSLY ESCAPED WITH MINOR INJURIES! AS FOR VICTOR VON DOOM...HIS FACE WAS HOPELESSLY DISFIGURED!!

VON DOOM, I AM EXPELLING YOU FROM THIS SCHOOL BEFORE YOU CAUSE GREATER HARM TO YOURSELF, OR TO US!!

BAH! THERE IS NOTHING MORE YOU CAN TEACH ME ANYWAY!

DAYS LATER, THE BANDAGES FINALLY COME OFF, AND THEN...

NO! NO! I'M UGLY!!! UGLY!! WHAT HAVE I DONE TO MYSELF?? WHAT HAVE I DONE..?! MY FACE IS TOO HORRIBLE! NO OTHER EYES MUST EVER GAZE UPON IT!! I'LL HIDE FROM THE SIGHT OF MANKIND --- SOMEWHERE... SOMEHOW!!

AND SO HE LEFT! HE TOOK HIMSELF TO THE REMOTE VASTNESS OF TIBET, SEEKING FORBIDDEN SECRETS OF BLACK MAGIC AND SORCERY!

FINALLY, HE WAS TAKEN IN BY A MYSTERIOUS ORDER OF MONKS WHO HAD DWELLED IN A LOST MOUNTAIN CAVE FOR CENTURIES!

AND THERE HE STAYED, MONTH AFTER MONTH, LEARNING THEIR ANCIENT SECRETS AND LORE, UNTIL THE DAY CAME WHEN THEY ADDRESSED HIM AS....

MASTER! ALL IS IN READINESS FOR YOU!

AND THEN IT BEGAN! USING THE MOUTH OF A GIGANTIC IDOL AS A MAKESHIFT BLAST FURNACE, THE TRAGIC, ILL-STARRED GYPSY BEGAN TO FORGE WHAT WAS SOON TO BE THE MOST DREADED COSTUME ON THE FACE OF THE EARTH!

MORE HEAT!! FIRE THE FURNACE!! DO YOU HEAR?? I MUST HAVE MORE HEAT!!

10.

EVENTUALLY, THE TASK WAS COMPLETED!

LET US KNOW IF IT PAINS YOU, MASTER!

PAIN?? THAT IS FOR *LESSER* MEN!! WHAT CAN PAIN MEAN TO VICTOR VON DOOM?!!

AND NOW... IT IS TIME FOR...*THE MASK!*

BUT, MASTER, IT HAS NOT COMPLETELY *COOLED* YET!

SAY NO MORE, MY BROTHER! HE WILL TOLERATE NO FURTHER DELAY! SUCH A MAN CANNOT WAIT, AS OTHERS CAN!

NEVER AGAIN WILL MORTAL EYES GAZE UPON THE HIDEOUS COUNTENANCE OF VICTOR VON DOOM!

FROM THIS MOMENT ON, THERE *IS* NO VICTOR VON DOOM! HE HAS VANISHED...ALONG WITH THE HANDSOME FACE HE ONCE POSSESSED! BUT, IN HIS PLACE, THERE SHALL BE ANOTHER...

...WISER...STRONGER! MORE BRILLIANT, MORE POWERFUL THAN EVER BEFORE!!

FROM THIS MOMENT ON, I SHALL BE KNOWN AS... *DOCTOR DOOM!*

ONLY *I* HAVE THE POWER TO REMOVE MY MASK... BY MANIPULATING THE MANY-FACETED RING UPON MY FINGER! AND NOW, THE FINAL PRECAUTION...

WE SHALL COVER YOUR RING WITH SPECIAL HERBS, CAMOUFLAGING IT SO COMPLETELY THAT NONE WILL SEE IT!!

YOU HAVE SERVED ME WELL...AS *ALL* MEN SHALL DO, ONE DAY! AND NOW, IT IS TIME TO ASSEMBLE MY GREATEST DISCOVERY...MY NUCLEAR-POWERED *FLYING HARNESS!*

11

"HE HAS LEFT US! WILL HE EVER RETURN?"

"NONE CAN TRULY SAY! FOR, SUCH A MAN MUST FOLLOW HIS DESTINY, NO MATTER WHERE IT MAY LEAD!"

"WOE TO THE WORLD, NOW THAT DOCTOR DOOM IS BORN!!"

AND HUMANITY SOON LEARNS, TO ITS SHOCKED DISMAY, OF THE AWESOME MENACE WHICH IS IN ITS MIDST....!

DAILY ALARUM
DOCTOR DOOM ISSUES ULTIMATUM TO EUROPE!

EVENING TR—
DOCTOR DOOM

THE POST
FANTASTIC FOUR IN NEW BATTLE WITH DOCTOR DOOM!

DOCTOR DOOM EVIL GENIUS CREATES NEW WEAPON

DAILY TELEG—
DOCTOR DOOM MAKES BID FOR POWER!

News—Record
DOCTOR DOOM WORLD MENACE!
FANTASTIC FOUR ASK PUBLIC NOT TO PANIC! GOVERNMENT ISSUES NEW REPORT!

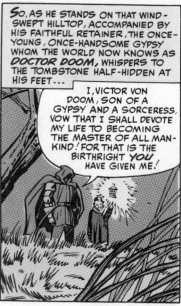

SO, AS HE STANDS ON THAT WIND-SWEPT HILLTOP, ACCOMPANIED BY HIS FAITHFUL RETAINER, THE ONCE-YOUNG, ONCE-HANDSOME GYPSY WHOM THE WORLD NOW KNOWS AS DOCTOR DOOM, WHISPERS TO THE TOMBSTONE HALF-HIDDEN AT HIS FEET...

I, VICTOR VON DOOM, SON OF A GYPSY AND A SORCERESS, VOW THAT I SHALL DEVOTE MY LIFE TO BECOMING THE MASTER OF ALL MANKIND! FOR THAT IS THE BIRTHRIGHT YOU HAVE GIVEN ME!

WITHOUT ANOTHER WORD, THE DRAMATIC BEING WHO HAS BECOME ABSOLUTE MONARCH OF THE KINGDOM OF LATVERIA, TURNS ON HIS HEEL AND WALKS THROUGH THE TINY VILLAGE, NEITHER SPEAKING NOR LOOKING LEFT NOR RIGHT!

GOOD DAY TO YOU, HERR DOCTOR!

MAY YOU ENJOY GOOD HEALTH, MASTER!

OURS HAS BEEN A PROSPEROUS LAND SINCE HE HAS RULED US!

MOMMY, LOOK! ISN'T THAT...?

HUSH, DEAR! YOU MUST BE SILENT WHEN THE MASTER PASSES!

AND SO, THE AWESOME FIGURE CONTINUES HIS WALK, SHOWING HIMSELF TO HIS SUBJECTS, WHILE HIS MIND DWELLS ON MATTERS WHICH ARE FAR BEYOND THEIR SIMPLE COMPREHENSION! AND THEN ...

NOW WE SHALL RETURN TO THE CASTLE!

YES, MASTER!

AGAIN HE LOCKS HIMSELF WITHIN HIS LABORATORY! AND, WHEN HE EMERGES ONCE MORE, WHO KNOWS WHAT NEW MENACE WILL HAVE BEEN CREATED, TO THREATEN MANKIND !??

THROUGH THE LONG, SILENT NIGHTS, IN THAT BARREN CASTLE, HALF-HIDDEN IN THE ISOLATED KINGDOM OF LATVERIA, DOCTOR DOOM WORKS, AND PLANS, AND BROODS! AND, WHEN HIS WORK IS FINALLY FINISHED...THEN LET THE WORLD BEWARE !!

12.

A DEMON—
FROM THE WORLD BEYOND!

Now take Dormammu, for instance. He posed a totally different sort of problem for us. What kind of problem? I'm glad you asked.

Dormammu was probably the first villain we created before the fact. What I mean is, we had been using his name for months as though he was somebody that everyone should know. I'd have Dr. Strange cry out things like "By the spell of the Dread Dormammu!" as easily as you might say "Make Mine Marvel!" We would refer to the Dark Domain of Dormammu, not because we had any idea what it was, or even where it was—but because I liked the way it sounded! I don't have to tell you how alliterative expletives and onomatopoeic incantations knock me out. Who can forget the deathless grandeur of "By the Hoary Hosts of Hoggoth!" or "By the Many Moons of Munnopor" (not to be confused with the equally imperishable "Mystic Moons of Munnopor")? You get the idea. But I never expected that I'd eventually have to create a Munnoporian Moon, or actually have to figure out who Hoggoth really was. See what we're leading up to?

Before I knew it, the mail started pouring in from Dr. Strange fanatics throughout the world (and the various dimensions and time warps thereof). It seems there was something about that nutty name, Dormammu, that was keeping Doc's devoted disciples awake nights trying to figure out who Dormammu was. I knew I was in big trouble. I had made up the name—now I had to dream up a character to go with the name. But who? But how?

Fortunately, I didn't have to face this pulse-pounding problem alone. In my time of trial, my hour of need, I knew I could count on Sturdy Steve Ditko for aid and comfort. Steve, as Marvelophiles everywhere will surely remember, was to the early, original Dr. Strange strips what Sherlock was to Holmes. Steve was both the illustrator and co-plotter of those first, fabulous issues, and there was no more talented delineatory teller of tales in the entire Marvel Bullpen. So, we got our heads together for a while and, flushed with the realization that the hovering hordes of fandom demanded the Dread Dormammu, we finally decreed, "Let there be Dormammu!"

Having decided to loose Dormammu upon the reading public, we then realized we were faced with a problem somewhat unusual even for us. Ever since I first coined his name, I constantly referred to ol' Dormy as "The Dweller of the Dark Domain" or "The Lord of the Realm of Darkness" or some such. Okay, that's easy enough to say. But now we had to show it. Think for a minute. How do you draw a "Dark Domain"? How do you portray a "Realm of Darkness"? Of course anyone else might have just drawn any old scene and merely added a lot of dark shadows. But we were Marvel men! Our public was counting on us! We knew we'd have to come up with a place that would look mystical . . . magical . . . menacing . . . and, most important of all . . . real! It would have to seem as though we had actually been there. After teasing the readers for issue after issue it was incumbent upon us to produce an environment for Dormammu that would exceed their wildest expectations. That was the challenge. And Steve answered it magnificently, as you soon shall see. The scenes and the settings looked so authentic, one would think that Mr. Ditko had actually just returned from there, and had been lucky enough to take a lot of photos for reference.

But what of Dormammu himself? How do you portray him who is "most powerful of the dwellers of the Realm of Darkness"? Steve had the answer for that one, too. He gave the demoniac D.D. (and we don't mean Daredevil!) a visage totally different from any villain I had ever seen in comics before. He gave him a face which was not a face—a head which is more than a head! You'd know he was Dormammu just by looking at him. Well, anyway, you'd know he certainly wasn't Irving Forbush!

Thus, Steve had designed just the villain we were looking for, and comfortably ensconced him in his own little free-form universe. But we weren't satisfied with that alone. We also added a mysterious captive female who would be destined to play a fateful role in the life of Dr. Strange as time went by. And even that wasn't enough.

56

Wait till you meet the Mindless Ones who both serve and threaten the Dread Dormammu. And, when it comes to mystic spells, you'll be reading enough incredible incantations to boggle the mind and bewilder the spirit. For, after all, we were attempting to create the first, the only, the most authentic comicbook series devoted to a master magician and his world of eerie enchantment.

But, at the time of Dormammu's creation, Dr. Strange had not yet been given an entire magazine of his own. Instead, he shared the limelight of our now-classical monthly publication *Strange Tales* with such other stellar features as The Human Torch and the blue-eyed Thing. Consequently, his first encounter with the Dread Dormammu was stretched over two issues, each part consisting of a ten-page installment. And, to show how we will do anything in the interest of accuracy, anything to keep these volumes historically pure, we have spared no effort, no expense, to bring you both chapters of the first fateful meeting of The Master of the Mystic Arts and The Dreaded Dweller of the Realm of Darkness, exactly as they first appeared in issues #126 and 127 of *Strange Tales,* published in the year 1964.

As another mighty Marvel bonus for you, both issues will be presented one after the other, with absolutely no commercial interruptions of any sort. Maybe television can't do it, but we can!

However, before we proceed with our portentous little playlet, I must caution you, one and all. When reading the mysterious invocations uttered by our hero and the dreaded one, we urge you to read them silently. Do not even move your lips. Let no sound escape you. For, so powerful and all-pervasive are these cataclysmic conjure chants that there's no way of predicting what might happen if you should accidentally mumble one with the wrong inflection—or when certain planets might be in a crucial configuration. Remember, in the world of Dr. Strange, we touch upon powers that the human mind can only begin to comprehend, powers that defy the rules of reason, the laws of earthly logic. Indeed, on the perilous pages ahead we enter the kingdom of the unknown, and we dare to tamper with forces that none may unleash—if the universe shall endure!

And so, the time has come. You are about to enter a fantastic galaxy of unbridled imageries, a nightmare arena of indescribable symbolism and awesome allegory. To usher you into this wonderment without end, there can be no better passwords than those contained within the spellbinding stanzas of Dr. Strange's favorite verse:

In the name of the All-Seeing
In the name of the All-Knowing
In the name of the All-Freeing
And the All-Bestowing
Though the Shadows now banish
My Amulet's light
In the name of Satannish
Protect us tonight!

Dr. STRANGE™ MASTER OF THE MYSTIC ARTS!

"THE DOMAIN OF THE DREAD DORMAMMU!"

THERE IS A WORLD HALF-HIDDEN BETWEEN THE REAL AND THE IMAGINARY!

IT IS TO THAT WORLD... THE WORLD OF MAGIC, THAT THIS TREND-SETTING SERIES IS DEDICATED!

WRITTEN BY: STAN LEE PRINCE OF PRESTIDIGITATORS!

ILLUSTRATED BY: STEVE DITKO LORD OF LEGERDEMAIN!

LETTERED BY: ART SIMEK NABOR OF NECROMANCY!

IT IS MIDNIGHT! THE CITY IS STILL! THE SILENCE IS THICK! THE SKY IS DARK AND STARLESS, AS THE ECTOPLASMIC FORM OF *DR. STRANGE* DRIFTS THRU HIS WINDOW TO REUNITE WITH HIS PHYSICAL FORM!

IT IS GOOD TO BE HOME AGAIN, NOW THAT I KNOW THE EVIL BARON MORDO HAS BEEN DEFEATED ONCE MORE!*

*SEE *STRANGE TALES* #125--EDITOR.

BUT, NO SOONER DOES THE MAN OF MYSTERY ATTAIN HIS MORTAL BODY, THAN HE FINDS HIMSELF IN THE GRIP OF A SPELL SO POWERFUL HE DARES NOT EVEN THINK ITS NAME!

ONLY ONE LIVING BEING HAS THE POWER TO *DO* THIS!! BUT-- *WHY??*

HALF WAY AROUND THE WORLD, IN WHAT SEEMS THE WINK OF AN EYE, DR. STRANGE RECEIVES HIS ANSWER...

I *KNEW* IT! IT IS THE *ANCIENT ONE!* BUT WHY DID YOU SUMMON ME, MASTER??

BECAUSE OF *HIM*-- THE ONE I NOW MAKE VISIBLE TO YOU!!

A *SPIRIT FORM!* DOES HE DARE TO MENACE *YOU*, MASTER??

NO, MY SON! HE IS MERELY A MESSENGER --FROM THE *DREAD DORMAMMU!!*

THE *DREAD DORMAMMU!!* MOST POWERFUL OF THE DWELLERS IN THE REALM OF DARKNESS!! WHAT DOES HE SEEK OF *US?*

HE THREATENS TO *LEAVE* THE DARK REALM--TO ENTER THE WORLD OF *MAN!* BUT THAT MUST NEVER *BE!*

HIS POWERS ARE TOO GREAT! HIS WAYS ARE TOO ALIEN! HUMANITY MUST NEVER BE THREATENED BY SUCH A MENACE! AND YET-- I AM TOO AGED--TOO WEARY-- TO STOP HIM!

SAY NO MORE, MASTER! *I* SHALL CONFRONT THE DREAD DORMAMMU!

2

REMEMBER THIS, MY SON-- HE IS LIKE NO FOE YOU HAVE EVER FOUGHT BEFORE! HIS POWER IS BEYOND DESCRIPTION-- HIS WORLD IS FRAUGHT WITH STRANGE DANGERS--

IT IS TRULY SAID --IN ALL THE UNIVERSE, THERE IS *NONE* SO TO COMPARE TO THE DREAD *DORMAMMU!*

EVEN *I*, AT THE HEIGHT OF MY POWER, WAS UNABLE TO DEFEAT HIM! IF YOU SHOULD FAIL-- THERE CAN BE NO HELP FOR YOU!!

I DARE *NOT* FAIL, MASTER!! TOO MUCH IS AT STAKE!!

SO *BE* IT, THEN!! BY THE SHADES OF THE SERAPHIM-- IN THE NAME OF THE ALL-SEEING AGAMOTTO--

-- I DISPATCH THEE TO-- *THE DOMAIN OF THE DREAD DORMAMMU!!!*

IT IS *DONE!!* THERE CAN BE NO TURNING BACK!! I AM COMMITTED TO THE BATTLE OF MY *LIFE!!*

SLOWLY THE MISTS BEGIN TO CLEAR, AS A STRANGE, STARTLING WORLD TAKES FORM! A WORLD IN WHICH THE IMPOSSIBLE IS BELIEVABLE, AND THE INCREDIBLE IS COMMONPLACE -- THE WORLD OF THE DARK DOMAIN-- THE WORLD OF THE DREAD *DORMAMMU!*

THE JOURNEY IS OVER! BUT, JUDGING BY THE UNSPEAKABLE MENACE I SEE BEFORE ME, THE *BATTLE* IS JUST BEGUN!

3

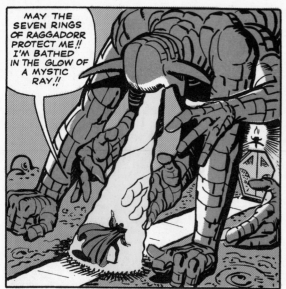

MAY THE SEVEN RINGS OF RAGGADORR PROTECT ME!! I'M BATHED IN THE GLOW OF A MYSTIC RAY!!

MY BRAIN IS ON FIRE! IT IS A TEST OF *WILL*-- AND *MINE* MUST PREVAIL!!

THE PAIN IS LESSENING!! I'VE *WON!* BEFORE ME A *DOOR* OPENS!

I HAVE NO CHOICE-- I MUST FOLLOW WHERE IT LEADS!

--AND, THOUGH IT LEADS TO THE DREAD *DORMAMMU* HIMSELF, I MUST NOT FALTER!!

BEHOLD, MASTER!! ONE COMES!!

HOW CAN THIS *BE??* IT IS *NOT* THE ANCIENT ONE!! IT IS MERELY HIS *DISCIPLE!!* VANQUISHING SO WEAK A FOE SHALL GIVE ME SMALL SATISFACTION!

THERE CAN BE BUT *ONE* ANSWER! THE ANCIENT ONE *KNOWS* I CANNOT BE STOPPED, SO HE DARES NOT COME HIMSELF! THE DIE IS CAST-- *EARTH SHALL SOON BE MINE!*

4

MASTER-- WHAT IF THE HUMAN BE **STRONGER** THAN YOU SUSPECT??

YOU **DARE** QUESTION **ME**-- THE DREAD DORMAMMU?!!

SUCH INSOLENCE MUST NOT GO UN- PUNISHED!!

NO, MASTER! **MERCY**-- WE BEG THEE--!!

WHAT DO **I** KNOW OF MERCY?? YOU SHALL REMAIN THUS IMPRISONED BY THE CRIMSON BANDS OF CYTTORAK TILL IT PLEASES ME TO RELEASE YOU!

MEANTIME, DR. STRANGE FACES HIS NEXT CHALLENGE... A MIDGET! HE APPEARS TO BE DEVOID OF POWER! AND YET, I MUST BE ON MY GUARD!

I'LL HOLD HIM AT BAY WITH A MILD SPELL AND THEN-- **WAIT!!** HE IS **GROWING** BEFORE MY EYES!!

I'LL NEED A **STRONGER** SPELL! BUT-- **AGAIN** HE HAS GROWN!!

NOW I SEE HIS POWER! HE **FEEDS** ON SPELLS! THEY **NOURISH** HIM!

'TIS **I** WHO HAVE MADE HIM GROW!!

NOW I MUST USE THE STRONGEST SPELL OF **ALL**--!

5

IT **WORKED!** PRAISE THE OMNIPOTENT OSHTUR! IT WAS **HE** WHO WARNED ME OF THOSE WHO **FEED** ON OTHER SPELLS!

BUT, **OTHER** EYES ARE WATCHING...

SO! **THAT** IS THE HUMAN CREATURE WHO DARES DEFY DORMAMMU!!

I HAVE HEARD FATHER SPEAK OF AN ANCIENT ONE WHO BATTLED DORMAMMU LONG AGO! IT CANNOT BE THE SAME ONE!

FOR **HE** IS YOUNG-- AND FAIR TO BEHOLD!

BUT **ALAS!** HE HAS BEEN SEIZED BY THE DWELLERS **BELOW!!**

I'M BEING DRAWN DOWN INTO THIS TWO-DIMENSIONAL OBJECT -- AS THOUGH SOME SORT OF LIFE EXISTS BELOW IT!!

HAH! WE HAVE FOUND ONE FROM ANOTHER DIMENSION! WHAT A **PRIZE** HE SHALL BE!!

I WAS **RIGHT!** IN THIS DARK DOMAIN, WORLDS WITHIN WORLDS EXIST!

BY THE TWELVE MOONS OF MUNNIPOR --THESE CREATURES CANNOT BE STOPPED BY **SPELLS!!** AND YET, THERE **MUST** BE A WAY--!!

6

OF *COURSE!!* THE ONE WEAPON WHICH NEVER FAILS ME!! MY ENCHANTED *AMULET!*

DWELLERS IN THE REALM OF DARKNESS CANNOT RESIST ITS GLEAMING, GLISTENING BEACON!!

THE CREATURE FROM ANOTHER WORLD POSSESSES COURAGE! WHAT A PITY HE CAN NEVER HOPE TO TRIUMPH OVER THE DREAD DORMAMMU!

WHY DOES HE CONTINUE ON?? SURELY BY NOW HE CAN SEE HOW *HOPELESS* IT IS!

BACK!! GO *BACK,* NOBLE HUMAN!

ODD-- I FEEL AS THOUGH I'M BEING *WATCHED* --AS THOUGH A VOICE INSIDE ME IS URGING ME TO GO *BACK!*

THEN, SUDDENLY...

ANOTHER DANGER! THE WORST- LOOKING SO FAR!

BY THE HOARY HOSTS OF HOGGOTH, THING OF EVIL-- *BEGONE!!!*

I DON'T *LIKE* IT! IT'S *TOO* EASY A VICTORY!

ANOTHER ONE! AND I'VE NO WAY OF KNOWING HOW MANY *MORE* WILL FOLLOW!

7

THE *BUBBLES* HE HAS THROWN ARE FORMING A POCKET AROUND ME!

NOW I KNOW WHY THE OTHER WAS SO EASY TO VANQUISH!! IT WAS TO THROW ME OFF-GUARD FOR THIS *NEW* MENACE!

I CANNOT BREAK FREE!! MY VERY SPELLS THEMSELVES SEEM UNABLE TO PENETRATE THIS AWESOME SCREEN!!

IT GROWS *THICKER*--MORE STIFLING!

BUT, IF I COULD CUT A *HOLE* IN THE SCREEN--A PATH FOR MY SPELLS TO GO THRU--ONCE *MORE* I MUST CALL UPON MY ENCHANTED AMULET!!

THERE! MY WAY IS *CLEAR* NOW!

FIRST, I LET THE LIGHT OF THE VISHANTI BATHE HIM IN ITS IRRESISTIBLE GLOW--

IMPRISONING HIM FOR AS LONG AS I DESIRE!

NEXT, I DISPEL THE POCKET AROUND ME--REPLACING IT WITH THE VAPORS OF VALTORR!!

AND NOW, THOUGH I SEE *OTHERS* ABOUT TO ASSAULT ME, I KNOW THAT I AM THEIR EQUAL--NAY, MORE THAN THAT-- I AM THEIR *SUPERIOR!*

NEVER HAVE I SEEN SUCH A ONE!! HE VANQUISHES THOSE WHO OPPOSE HIM AS IF HE'S THE DREAD DORMAMMU *HIMSELF!*

8

AND, AT THAT VERY INSTANT, THE MONARCH OF THE DARK DOMAIN GIVES VENT TO HIS UNCONTROLLABLE RAGE--

SO! YOU ALLOWED YOURSELVES TO BE DEFEATED BY A LONE INTRUDER!!

MERCY, MASTER! WE DID OUR BEST!

SILENCE!! I BANISH YOU ALL TO LIMBO! THE VERY SIGHT OF YOU IS OFFENSIVE TO MY EYES!

WHEN THE INTRUDER IS SLAIN, YOU SHALL RETURN! BUT, NOT AN INSTANT BEFORE!

AND NOW, I MYSELF SHALL DEAL WITH THE ONE FROM THE WORLD CALLED EARTH! LET HIM BE BROUGHT TO ME!!

NO SOONER HAS THE THOUGHT TAKEN FORM, THAN A MYSTIC PATH APPEARS, LEADING TO THE DREAD DORMAMMU!

NEVER HAVE I SENSED SUCH RAGE, SUCH FURY IN THE HEART OF DORMAMMU! THE VALIANT STRANGER WALKS TO HIS DOOM!!

COME FORWARD, YOU OF THE OUTER WORLD!! I WISH TO LOOK UPON YOUR FEATURES--BEFORE YOU DIE!

I SENSE SOMEONE BEHIND ME! I WAS RIGHT! IT'S--A GIRL!

STOP! YOU MUST GO NO FURTHER! THE DREAD DORMAMMU WAITS TO SLAY YOU!

I AM AWARE OF THAT!

BUT YOU CANNOT SUSPECT HOW POWERFUL HE IS! YOU THROW AWAY YOUR LIFE BY FACING HIM!

9

OUR MYSTICAL SAGA BEGINS IN A DIMENSION SO ALIEN, SO INCREDIBLE, SO UTTERLY BEYOND HUMAN COMPREHENSION, THERE ARE NO WORDS IN ANY EARTHLY LANGUAGE TO ACCURATELY DESCRIBE IT! FOR THIS IS THE DIMENSION OF THE DREAD DORMAMMU... AND IT IS HERE THAT OUR TALE BEGINS...

I *WARN* YOU TO SEND THE *ANCIENT ONE* TO FIGHT IN YOUR STEAD! YOU ARE TOO YOUNG... YOUR KNOWLEDGE OF THE MYSTIC ARTS CANNOT BEGIN TO EQUAL *MINE*!

NO, DREADED ONE! IT IS *ME* WHOM THE ANCIENT ONE HAS SENT... AND IT IS *ME* WHOM YOU MUST BATTLE!

BAH! ALL THROUGH THE AGES, WITLESS CREATURES SUCH AS YOU HAVE DARED TO CHALLENGE ME... AND ALL HAVE MET THE SAME DEADLY FATE! I SHALL GIVE YOU A BRIEF PERIOD TO RECONSIDER BEFORE I SUMMON YOU TO YOUR FINAL BATTLE!

FOR I NO LONGER DERIVE *PLEASURE* FROM DEFEATING WEAK OPPONENTS ... THE SPORT NOW BORES ME!

AND SO, MOMENTS LATER...

HE SOUNDED SO SURE OF HIMSELF... SO TOTALLY ARROGANT! CAN HE *REALLY* BE SO COMPLETELY UNBEATABLE!?

THEN, SUDDENLY, THE MYSTERIOUS FEMALE WHO HAD TRIED TO WARN DR. STRANGE WHEN HE ENTERED THE DREAD DIMENSION AGAIN APPEARS...

HEED MY WORDS, MAN FROM ANOTHER WORLD! YOU MUST NOT BATTLE DORMAMMU!

YOU WASTE YOUR BREATH! *NOTHING* CAN STOP ME! I MUST SAVE HUMANITY FROM THE DREADED ONE!

EVEN THOUGH I *PERISH* IN THE ATTEMPT, I DARE NOT FALTER! MY LIFE MEANS NOTHING!

NO! IT IS NOT ONLY OF *YOU* I AM THINKING! IF, BY SOME UNBELIEVABLE MIRACLE YOU SHOULD *TRIUMPH*, IT COULD MEAN THE END OF *US*!

I DO NOT UNDERSTAND!

THEN YOU MUST BE *SHOWN!* PREPARE YOURSELF, EARTH MORTAL... PREPARE FOR SIGHTS SUCH AS NO HUMAN EYES HAVE EVER BEFORE BEHELD!

LET THE *ENTRANCE* APPEAR... THE ENTRANCE TO... THE *BEYOND!*

AND NOW, FOLLOW ME... AND BE PREPARED TO WITNESS THE INCREDIBLE!

I MUST BE VIGILANT... IT MIGHT BE A TRAP! AND YET, MY INSTINCTS TELL ME SHE IS SINCERE!

2.

SECONDS LATER, THE EARTHBORN MASTER OF BLACK MAGIC WITNESSES SIGHTS WHICH STRAIN HIS SHOCKED SENSES TO THE BREAKING POINT!

THIS IS BUT THE *START* OF THE EERIE SPECTACLE YOU ARE ABOUT TO SEE...!

FOR, THIS IS THE OUTSKIRTS OF DORMAMMU'S DOMAIN... WHERE THE MINDLESS ONES DWELL!

THE *MINDLESS ONES* ??!

YES! AND THERE THEY *ARE*...PRIMITIVE, SAVAGE, TOTALLY DEVOID OF LOVE, OR KINDNESS, OR ANY TYPE OF INTELLIGENCE! THEY LIVE ONLY TO *FIGHT*... AND TO DESTROY!

THEY HAVE LIVED AT THE FRINGE OF OUR DIMENSION SINCE THE BEGINNING OF TIME... EVER WAITING FOR A CHANCE TO ATTACK US...TO SLAY US ALL!

LOOK OUT! WE VENTURED TOO CLOSE! THEY HAVE *SEEN* US! QUICK... FOLLOW ME!

WHY HAVE THEY NEVER CONQUERED YOU BEFORE? WHAT HAS *STOPPED* THEM ??

3.

ONLY *ONE* THING...THIS MYSTIC SHIELD BEHIND WHICH WE BOTH HAVE RUN! IT IS TOO POWERFUL FOR THE MINDLESS ONES TO PENETRATE!

IT WAS CREATED BY *DORMAMMU*, AGES AGO...TO KEEP US SAFE FROM THOSE WHO WOULD DESTROY US!

ONLY THE MIGHTY SPELLS OF THE DREADED ONE CAN KEEP THE SHIELD IN EXISTENCE! IF ANYTHING SHOULD HAPPEN TO *HIM*, THEN ALL OF US HERE IN HIS DIMENSION ARE *DOOMED!*

I KNOW THAT SHE SPEAKS THE TRUTH! IT IS NO TRICK! THOUGH HE REPRESENTS A MENACE TO *MAN-KIND*, DORMAMMU IS A PROTECTOR TO HIS *OWN* PEOPLE!

THAT IS WHY YOU MUST NOT DEFEAT HIM! ONLY *HE* CAN SAVE US FROM THE MINDLESS ONES!

YET, IF HE LIVES, *HUMANITY* SHALL ALWAYS BE IN DANGER!

I WISH TO BRING NO HARM TO THIS FANTASTIC WORLD... AND YET MY FIRST DUTY IS TO EARTH... AND THE ONES WHO INHABIT IT!

I HAVE NO CHOICE... I MUST BE TRUE TO MY OATH!

THEN, FINALLY... AND BLOOD! THE TIME IS *HERE!*

COME, MAN OF FLESH

DORMAMMU'S SUMMONS! NOW, THE DIE IS CAST!

THE *GIRL!* WHAT HAVE YOU *DONE* TO HER??

SHE *KNEW* THE PENALTY FOR SPEAKING TO AN ENEMY! SHE HAS *BETRAYED* ME... AND SO, HER FATE IS NOW LINKED WITH *YOURS!*

BUT... SHE MERELY TRIED TO *HELP* ...! TO CONVINCE ME NOT TO FIGHT...!

SILENCE! FIRST, SHE SHALL WITNESS *YOUR* DEFEAT...THEN, SHE SHALL BE *NEXT* TO DIE! *DORMAMMU HAS SPOKEN!*

NOW, LET THE BATTLE BEGIN! THE BATTLE WHICH SHALL END AS ALL THOSE IN THE PAST... WITH THE COMPLETE VICTORY OF *DORMAMMU*, MASTER OF THE DARK DOMAIN!

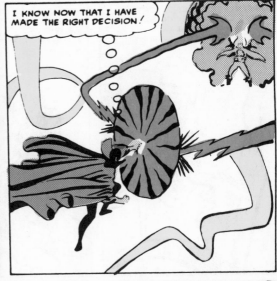

I KNOW NOW THAT I HAVE MADE THE RIGHT DECISION!

NO MATTER WHAT THE CONSEQUENCES, DORMAMMU IS TOO POWERFUL, TOO EVIL, TO BE ALLOWED TO EXIST!

NO MATTER WHAT THE COST... NO MATTER WHAT THE CONSEQUENCES...HE MUST BE *DESTROYED!*

HE IS MERELY TOYING WITH ME NOW...TESTING MY DEFENSES! TRYING TO CONFUSE AND BEWILDER ME!

BUT, HE SHALL SEE THAT I, *TOO*, HAVE MAGICAL WEAPONS!

I, *TOO*, CAN CAST SPELLS WHICH HAVE THE POWER TO CONFOUND AND TO DAZZLE!

SO, HUMAN! YOU ARE A MORE CAPABLE FOE THAN I SUSPECTED! ALL THE MORE PITY THAT I SHALL BE FORCED TO VANQIIISH YOU!

5.

OBSERVE, HELPLESS MORTAL, HOW I CAN MAKE YOU SLOWLY FADE AWAY TO SHEER NOTHINGNESS!

WITHIN A FEW BRIEF SECONDS YOU SHALL BE GONE... FOREVER!

NEVER, DORMAMMU! NOT WHILE THE HOARY HOSTS OF HOGGOTH ARE MINE TO COMMAND!

FOR, THOUGH YOU MOCK THE EARTHLY POWERS I POSSESS, THEY STILL SHALL PROVE EQUAL TO THE TASK OF DEFEATING YOU!

I SEE YOU ARE SURPRISED TO SEE ME SHRUG OFF YOUR FATAL SPELL! WELL, HERE IS YET ANOTHER SURPRISE FOR YOU....!

BAH! A MERE CONJURER'S CONE! I DABBLED WITH SUCH PUNY TRICKS WHEN I WAS BUT A CHILD!

YOU STILL CANNOT EVEN BEGIN TO COMPREHEND THE SCOPE AND EXTENT OF MY ALMOST LIMITLESS POWERS!

AND SO THE BATTLE RAGES... A BATTLE BETWEEN TWO TOTALLY ALIEN FOES... FOES WITH ONLY ONE THING IS COMMON... AN AWESOME MASTERY OF THE POWERS OF BLACK MAGIC!

WHILE, IN A SILENT RETREAT IN TIBET, AN AGED MYSTIC OBSERVES EVERY DETAIL OF THE FATEFUL CONFRONTATION... FOR THIS IS... THE ANCIENT ONE!

THERE IS NO TURNING BACK NOW! THE GAME MUST BE PLAYED TO THE END!

MAY THE LIGHT OF THE VISHANTI SHINE UPON DR. STRANGE... AND MAY THE OMNIPOTENT OSHTUR GRANT HIM WISDOM AND STRENGTH!

6.

74

MEANWHILE...

HIS ATTACK GROWS EVER STRONGER!

AND, TRY AS I MAY, I CANNOT BREAK THROUGH HIS DEFENSES... I CANNOT FIND A WAY TO *REACH* HIM!

WHILE THE ALIEN BRAIN OF DORMAMMU IS THINKING...

I AM STRONGER THAN HE... BUT NEVER BEFORE HAVE I SEEN SUCH COURAGE...SUCH VALOR!

BUT, NEITHER COURAGE NOR VALOR ALONE ARE ENOUGH TO PREVAIL AGAINST MY SUPERIOR MIGHT!

THE ULTIMATE VICTORY *MUST* BE MINE! THERE CAN BE NO OTHER OUTCOME! IT IS ONLY A MATTER OF TIME!

MEANWHILE, THE HELPLESS GIRL WATCHES, WITH FEARFUL EYES...

IT MATTERS NOT *WHO* SHALL WIN! IN ANY EVENT *I* AM DOOMED!

HIS POWER CONTINUES TO INCREASE, WHILE MINE GROWS WEAKER! WHAT MANNER OF BEING *IS* HE? IS THERE *NO* WAY TO DRAIN HIS STRENGTH??

BUT, I MUST NOT ALLOW MY MIND TO DWELL ON THOUGHTS OF DEFEAT! I MUST FIGHT ON...UNTIL THE END!

IT WILL SOON BE OVER! THE MORTAL ONE CANNOT HOLD OUT MUCH LONGER!

7.

75

BUT, UNKNOWN TO EITHER COMBATANT, WHILE THE DREAD DORMAMMU EXERTS MORE AND MORE ENERGY TO DEFEAT HIS MORTAL FOE, HIS *BARRIER SHIELD* GETS PROGRESSIVELY *WEAKER*, AS THE MINDLESS ONES SLOWLY REALIZE...

SEEING A FEW LEADERS SHUFFLING THROUGH THE BARRIER, *OTHERS* SOON FOLLOW...

UNTIL A VASTE, ONRUSHING *HORDE* OF SAVAGE, RUTHLESS CREATURES SPILL OVER INTO THE DOMAIN OF THE DREAD DORMAMMU!

THE *MINDLESS ONES!* THEY'VE *BROKEN THROUGH!* NOW *NOTHING* MATTERS! WE ARE ALL DOOMED!

DORMAMMU HAS HALTED HIS ATTACK ON ME! *WHY???*

I SHALL ATTEND TO YOU *LATER*, EARTHLING! FOR THE MOMENT, I SEE A MORE PRESSING PROBLEM TO DISPOSE OF!

HE HAS TURNED HIS BACK TO ME! THIS IS MY CHANCE! AND YET... I CANNOT DO BATTLE IN SUCH A MANNER!

BACK, CREATURES OF THE NIGHT!!!... BACK... I *COMMAND* YOU, BY THE SEVEN RINGS OF RAGGADORR!

MY EMERGENCY BARRIER SHIELD IS NOT STRONG ENOUGH! THEY ADVANCE TOO QUICKLY! I CANNOT HOLD THEM ALL BACK!

8.

IF DORMAMMU IS UNABLE TO STOP THE MINDLESS ONES, THEN ALL WHO DWELL IN THIS DARK DIMENSION WILL BE *SLAIN!*

MANY ARE INNOCENT... UNDESERVING OF SUCH A FATE! THEY MUST BE SAVED!

HIS POWER MUST BE INCREASED! PERHAPS, IF I BATHE HIM IN THE LIGHT OF MY ENCHANTED AMULET...!

STAND *STILL,* DREADED ONE! LET THE POWER OF MY AMULET SEEP INTO YOU, ADDING TO YOUR OWN!

THEN, FORTIFIED BY AWESOME ENERGY FROM DR. STRANGE'S GLEAMING JEWEL, DORMAMMU FINDS HIS STRENGTH INCREASING, UNTIL...

THEY CANNOT PENETRATE ANY FURTHER! IT *HOLDS!* MY BARRIER *HOLDS!*

BUT, INSTEAD OF WORDS OF GRATITUDE, DORMAMMU EXPRESSES *RAGE...!*

CURSE YOU, MORTAL! CURSE THE FACT THAT I NEEDED YOUR HELP! CURSE THE WOEFUL FATE THAT HAD PLACED ME IN YOUR DEBT! I CANNOT SLAY YOU NOW! I CANNOT DESTROY THE ONE WHO HAS SAVED ME!

IT IS AS I SUSPECTED! HE IS EVIL, TRUE... BUT ONLY BY OUR *HUMAN* STANDARDS! ACCORDING TO HIS *OWN* LIGHTS, HE HAS HIS OWN MORAL CODE!

TRULY, YOU *ARE* IN MY DEBT, DORMAMMU! BUT, I SHALL GO EASY ON YOU! I ASK ONLY *TWO* PROMISES... AND THEN, THE DEBT SHALL BE *PAID!* ONE: NO HARM MUST COME TO THIS FEMALE! *TWO:* YOU MUST VOW NEVER TO INVADE THE EARTH!

SO *BE* IT! EVEN THOUGH I AM YOUR SUPERIOR, YOU HAVE DONE WHAT NONE COULD DO SINCE TIME IMMEMORIAL... YOU HAVE *DEFEATED* DORMAMMU! BUT, I SHALL NEVER REST UNTIL I HAVE *AVENGED* THIS INDIGNITY!

WHAT WILL BECOME OF *YOU,* NOW? PERHAPS THERE COULD BE A WAY TO TAKE YOU *BACK* WITH ME!?

NO, THIS IS MY WORLD! IT IS *HERE* THAT I BELONG... NO MATTER WHERE MY *HEART* SHALL BE!

GO, MAN OF MYSTERY, AND WHATEVER BEFALLS, ALWAYS KNOW... I SHALL NEVER FORGET YOU!

IT MIGHT BE A SECOND LATER, OR A YEAR...FOR, HOW CAN ONE MEASURE TIME IN THE MYSTIC REALM BETWEEN DIMENSIONS?? BUT, NO MATTER *WHEN* IT IS, UPON REACHING THE RETREAT OF THE ANCIENT ONE, DR. STRANGE FINDS...

MY MASTER IS *GONE!* BUT...WHERE...??

HERE, MY DEVOTED DISCIPLE! HERE IS THE ONE WHOSE HEART IS FILLED WITH *PRIDE* AT YOUR VICTORY!

MASTER! YOU SEEM *STRONGER...* MORE ROBUST THAN I HAVE EVER SEEN YOU! HOW EFFORTLESSLY YOU ATTAIN THE FLOATING POSITION OF *NIRVANA!*

THAT IS BECAUSE OF YOUR DEED, MY SON! YOUR TRIUMPH OVER DORMAMMU HAS BROKEN THE SPELL WHICH *HE* HAD PLACED ON ME, AGES AGO!

AND NOW, IT IS TIME FOR YOU TO RECEIVE YOUR *REWARD...* SEE WHAT I BESTOW UPON THEE!

FROM THIS MOMENT FORTH, YOU SHALL HAVE A *NEW* CAPE, AND A MORE WONDROUS AMULET!

YOU SHALL *NEED* NEW POWERS, FOR YOU WILL BE CALLED UPON TO PERFORM EVEN *GREATER* DEEDS IN THE FUTURE!

I PRAY THAT I BE FOUND *WORTHY*, MASTER!

YOU HAVE *ALREADY* BEEN FOUND WORTHY, LOYAL ONE! FOR, IT IS *YOU* WHO SHALL REPLACE ME WHEN THE TIME COMES FOR ME TO BREATHE THE FINAL VAPORS OF VALTORR! IT IS *YOU* WHO SHALL ONE DAY BECOME... THE *MASTER!*

AND, I PRAY THAT THE AWESOME WEIGHT OF THE RESPONSIBILITY, AND THE UNIMAGINABLE LONELINESS WILL NOT BE MORE THAN HE CAN BEAR!

DR. STRANGE WILL THRILL AND AMAZE YOU AGAIN *NEXT* ISSUE! TILL THEN, MAY YOU AND YOUR LOVED ONES BATHE IN THE LIGHT OF THE VISHANTI!

The End

10.

IF A GOD BE MAD!

And now we get into the heavy stuff!

Where can you go after you've dealt with a Latverian king and a Ruler of the Dark Dimension? Asgard is as good a place as any, right? Right! So buckle your seat belt, pilgrim, we're on our way!

In Volume One of this somewhat cerebral series, *Origins of Marvel Comics,* we learned how the lame and laconic Dr. Don Blake was startlingly transformed into the mighty Thor, God of Thunder, due to a supernatural accident. We were privileged to visit Asgard, home of the legendary Norse Gods, and to meet Thor's friends and his immediate family. We learned of the fabled Rainbow Bridge, the ubiquitous Uru hammer, and all the other delicious details which have made Asgard freaks of countless millions. We also met Balder the Brave and the stunning Sif, a goddess who can really hack it. But, through a grievous oversight, we neglected to introduce you to one of the most crucially important characters in the entire series. We're speaking, of course, of Loki, God of Evil! Loki, the Thunder God's stepbrother (or is it half-brother? I never get it right). Loki, villainy incarnate—doer of a thousand dastardly deeds!

However, though we've been known to make a rare omission or two, let no man say that the lustrous legions of Marveldom do not hasten to correct so gross a misdeed. Hence, on the pages that follow, you shall not only meet the sinister second son of Odin, but you shall observe, with your own awestruck eyes, the memorable tales that depict his childhood and trace the development of his burgeoning hatred for mighty Thor.

Though Jolly Jack Kirby acted as wardrobe master for our Asgardian assemblage, neither he nor I actually created the character Loki. For Loki, as you know, is as much a part of Norse mythology as omnipotent Odin and Bifrost itself. As a matter of fact, I've always sort of thought of Thor and Loki as resembling, in a distant way, the biblical Cain and Abel, except that Thor so far has managed to survive Loki's lethal little attacks.

You know, writing comicbook stories really isn't all that much different from writing any other type of adventure saga. You create a hero for yourself, hoping that the reader will identify with him and care about him. Then you dig up a villain, find a way to motivate him, set the stage, and let them go! But, as any serious scholar of Marvel mythos is sure to have observed, the key phrase is "motivate him." More stories have been ruined, more plots have been diluted, because of villains who were improperly motivated or not really motivated at all. Too many times a villain simply attacks the hero for the same reason men have given for climbing mountains—because they're there. One reason I chose the leering Loki to be the Thunder God's main antagonist is because it was possible to give him so compelling a motive for hating Thor and for continually plotting his brother's downfall. The jealousy of one prince for another! Sibling rivalry between two gods! Those are motives that anyone can accept and understand, motives worthy of ancient Greek drama, or enduring Shakespearian tragedy—or Marvel Comics!

Another factor that seemed to make Loki the perfect archenemy for Goldilocks is the fact that both have godly powers. And, though Thor possesses greater physical strength than the God of Evil, Loki more than compensates by his mastery of deadly spells and savage sorcery. Storybook battles are always far more interesting and far more effective when the opponents seem to be evenly matched—or when the villain actually appears to be the stronger. And, since Loki is ever the schemer, ever the plotter, ever the precipitator of each fateful encounter, he usually enters the fray with the scales of battle tipped precariously in his favor.

As in the case of Dr. Doom, we had been featuring Loki for quite a few years (The Mighty Thor actually first saw print in *Journey into Mystery* #83, dated August 1962) before we realized that we had never done an origin story about Odin's bad boy. In fact, come to think of it, I can't remember doing an origin story about Thor himself, or Odin, or Balder, or even Volstagg—but that's neither here nor there. I wanted to do a bit about Loki because I felt we had the perfect place to put it. And, now that I've slyly piqued your interest...

We had been running a little five-page featurette in *Journey into Mystery* in '63 and '64 called "Tales of Asgard." It gave Jack a chance to really do some impressive larger-size artwork, since he only averaged about four panels per page, as contrasted to the five or six panels he'd employ in the regular Thor stories. Also, it enabled us to give our readers a better insight into the Asgardian legends, both the ones we gleaned from Norse mythology and the ones we created ourselves, loosely based on what had gone before. We've always felt we have a perfect right to embellish the old legends, and create our own. After all, the Odyssey and the Iliad were probably the Marvel Comics of their day. But I fear I digress.

It occurred to me that our "Tales of Asgard" feature would be the perfect showcase for a graphic depiction of Loki's childhood and his growing hatred for Thor. So once again Jack and I put our heads together (while he almost poked out my eye with his fershlugginer cigar), and lo, another origin tale was born!

But, for the uncounted thousands of you who are using this death-less dissertation as the theme for a college term paper, it behooves me—in the interest of precision and accuracy—to mention the following vital technical minutiae. The burgeoning bio of Loki which you're about to peruse and treasure was much too long to fit into a five-page featurette. Therefore, Jack and I extended it over three issues of *Journey into Mystery*. (Obviously, this happened some time before we decided to change the name of the magazine to *The Mighty Thor*.) It began in issue #112 and was entitled "The Coming of Loki." Then it was followed, in #113, with "The Boyhood of Loki." But pay attention now—here's where it gets hairy. The third and final portion of our semi-saga didn't ever appear in issue #114! It skipped that issue and finally thrilled a breathlessly waiting world in ish #115. Why? We might as well level with you. When writing #114 . . . we just plain forgot about it! It wasn't till the next issue that I mentioned to Jack, "Hey, did we ever do the wrap-up of Loki's origin?" The look on his face was all the answer that I needed! Now remember—you have just shared a secret with us that no one in the outside world has ever been privy to. Guard it well, O True Believer. You are now deep within the charmed Asgardian circle—may Odin shower the blessings of peace and wisdom upon thine honored brow!

And now, prepare for battle beyond belief, for panorama to quicken your pulse and spectacle to leave you breathless. You are about to witness Lord Odin himself in battle against the giant King of Jotunheim—and that's only the beginning. In the pages that follow, we present a cast of thousands; but, even more important, we present the way in which Loki came to be recognized as half-brother to Thor. That was the start of it—the terrible moment that was to bring all who live to the very brink of Ragnarok itself!

THE START OF A NEW MARVEL BIOGRAPHY-IN-DEPTH...

Tales of ASGARD HOME OF THE MIGHTY NORSE GODS!

"THE COMING OF LOKI!"

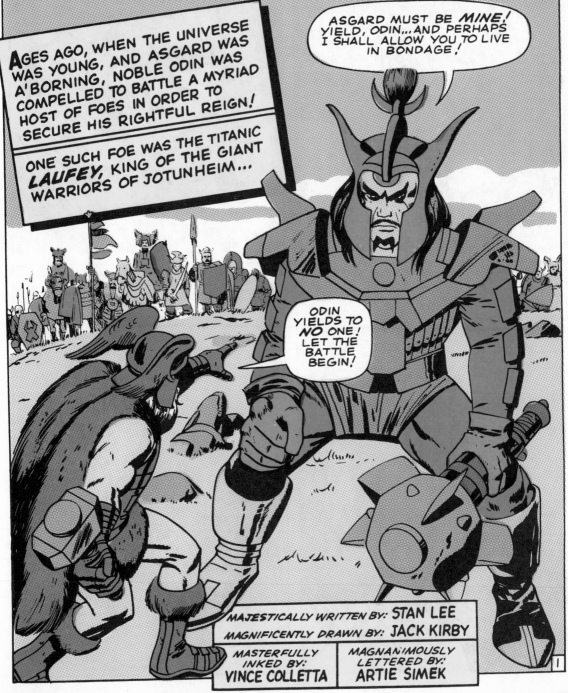

AGES AGO, WHEN THE UNIVERSE WAS YOUNG, AND ASGARD WAS A'BORNING, NOBLE ODIN WAS COMPELLED TO BATTLE A MYRIAD HOST OF FOES IN ORDER TO SECURE HIS RIGHTFUL REIGN!

ONE SUCH FOE WAS THE TITANIC *LAUFEY*, KING OF THE GIANT WARRIORS OF JOTUNHEIM...

ASGARD MUST BE *MINE!* YIELD, ODIN...AND PERHAPS I SHALL ALLOW YOU TO LIVE IN BONDAGE!

ODIN YIELDS TO *NO* ONE! LET THE BATTLE BEGIN!

MAJESTICALLY WRITTEN BY: STAN LEE

MAGNIFICENTLY DRAWN BY: JACK KIRBY

MASTERFULLY INKED BY: VINCE COLLETTA

MAGNANIMOUSLY LETTERED BY: ARTIE SIMEK

1

IT WILL TAKE NO MORE THAN *ONE BLOW* OF MY THUNDERING WAR CLUB TO---*HOLD, ODIN!* STAND YOUR GROUND AND *FIGHT!*

I *STAND* MY GROUND! BUT YOUR MOVEMENTS ARE CLUMSY-- YOUR ARM IS SLOW!

HOWEVER, LAUFEY'S POUNDING WAR CLUB EVENTUALLY *DOES* FIND ITS TARGET, AS DOES ODIN'S LEGENDARY HAMMER--AND THE BATTLE IS ON, AS THE VERY PEAKS OF JOTUNHEIM RING WITH THE SOUND OF THE EPIC DUEL!

I NO LONGER HEAR YOUR EMPTY BOASTS, KING OF JOTUNHEIM! DOES THE POWER OF MY HAMMER *SURPRISE* YOU??

AYE, BEARDED ONE! BUT YOUR VALOR IS WASTED UPON A BATTLE YOU CAN NEVER HOPE TO WIN!

KNOW YOU, THIS LAND IS *MINE!* SEE HOW I ALMOST CAUSED YOU TO STEP ON A FATAL POTHOLE WHICH POURS FORTH COSMIC FLAME!

HIS WORDS RING *TRUE!* IN THIS ALIEN LAND, THE ADVANTAGE IS *HIS*--UNLESS I CAN ACHIEVE VICTORY WITHIN *MINUTES!*

2

ENOUGH OF THIS USELESS DUEL! LET THE DECISION BE *NOW*! HAVE YOU FORGOTTEN, SAVAGE LAUFEY, A HAMMER CAN BE *THROWN* AS WELL AS SWUNG??!

MY WAR CLUB-- *SHATTERED*!

SEEING THEIR MONARCH'S WEAPON SO EASILY DESTROYED, THE GIANT WARRIORS OF JOTUNHEIM BELLOW IN UNCONTROLLABLE RAGE, AS THEY BREAK RANKS, HUNGERING TO JOIN THE BATTLE!

DEATH TO ALL THE MINIONS OF ASGARD! THEY MUST BE CRUSHED FOR THE GLORY OF JOTUNHEIM!

WE CAN REMAIN IN-ACTIVE NO LONGER! OUR WARLORD IS DEFENSELESS! WE MUST FIGHT AT THE SIDE OF LAUFEY!

STRIKE FOR JOTUNHEIM! SLAY THE WARRIORS OF ASGARD!

THEN, SOUNDING THEIR EAR-SHATTERING WAR CRY, PLACING A POWERFUL BATTLE-SWORD IN THE EAGER HAND OF LAUFEY, THE ENTIRE ASSEMBLED FIGHTING FORCE OF JOTUNHEIM SURGES FORWARD LIKE AN IRRESISTIBLE LIVING TIDAL WAVE....!

YOUR SWORD, MY KING! MAY IT POINT THE WAY TO *VICTORY*!

TO MY *SIDE*, WARRIORS OF ASGARD! LET THE STRENGTH OF OUR LIMBS, THE POWER OF OUR ARMS, DRIVE BACK THE HORDES OF LAUFEY!

3

THERE ARE NO EARTHLY WORDS WHICH CAN ADEQUATELY DESCRIBE A BATTLE SUCH AS THIS! SO WE, POOR MORTALS, WILL NOT EVEN ATTEMPT SUCH A DESCRIPTION! WE SHALL MERELY ALLOW THE SCENE TO SPEAK FOR ITSELF!

TO FOES SUCH AS THESE-- IN A CONFLICT SUCH AS THIS--TIME HAS LITTLE OR NO MEANING! IT MIGHT BE MINUTES, HOURS, OR DAYS--BUT FINALLY, THE COURAGE AND THE SKILL OF ODIN'S LEGIONS SERVE TO DRIVE BACK LAUFEY'S BEATEN WARRIORS, IN ONE OF THE GREATEST VICTORIES IN THE ANNALS OF ASGARD!

FLEE! WE CAN FIGHT NO LONGER! THE CAUSE IS LOST! ODIN HAS TRIUMPHED AGAIN!

NO! I ORDER DEATH TO THOSE WHO SURRENDER! WE SHALL REGROUP AT MY CASTLE, AND ATTACK AGAIN--WHEN THEY LEAST SUSPECT IT!

BUT ODIN, EVER VIGILANT, EVER OMNIPOTENT, HAS HEARD LAUFEY'S DESPERATE CRY, AND SO A NEW ORDER IS ISSUED BY THE MIGHTY MONARCH...!

AFTER THEM! THE REIGN OF LAUFEY MUST BE ENDED FOREVER! SO LONG AS HE IS KING OF JOTUNHEIM, OUR VICTORY WILL NEVER BE COMPLETE!

4

BUT, LAUFEY'S COURAGE IS A MATCH FOR HIS AMBITION--AND HE CHOOSES DEATH AT THE HANDS OF HIS ENEMY RATHER THAN THE IGNOMINY OF SURRENDER!

ENOUGH! LET THE FIGHTING CEASE! THE WARLORD OF JOTUNHEIM IS SLAIN!

SOMETHING LIVES WITHIN THAT BUNDLE! OPEN IT, THAT I MAY BEHOLD ITS CONTENT!

I HEAR A FAINT WHIMPERING CRY! METHINKS, MY LORD, THERE IS AN INFANT CHILD WITHIN!

OF COURSE! IT IS LOKI, SON OF LAUFEY! THE CHILD HE KEPT HIDDEN, FOR HIS HEART WAS FILLED WITH SHAME THAT LOKI WAS NOT BORN A GIANT, AS WERE THE OTHER OFFSPRING OF JOTUNHEIM!

LOKI! THE VERY NAME HAS A RING OF EVIL -- A TINGE OF FOREBODING TO IT!

MAYHAP! BUT STILL HE IS A REGAL PRINCE, SON OF A KINGLY FATHER! I MUST ACCORD HIM HIS RIGHTFUL DUE!

HEAR ME, LEGIONS OF ASGARD! FROM THIS MOMENT HENCE, I PROCLAIM LOKI: SON OF ODIN, HALF-BROTHER TO MY WELL-BELOVED THOR! FOR BETTER OR FOR WORSE, LOKI IS FOREVERMORE AN IMMORTAL OF ASGARD! THIS HAVE I PROCLAIMED! SO BE IT!

MANY ARE THE LEGENDS OF LOKI'S BIRTH -- BUT THIS IS ONE WE FAVOR! HOWEVER, WE HAVE MERELY SCRATCHED THE SURFACE -- WE HAVE BARELY BEGUN THIS DRAMATIC BIOGRAPHY-IN-DEPTH! IN FORTHCOMING ISSUES, WE SHALL TRACE LOKI'S EARLY CHILDHOOD -- AND YOU SHALL RELIVE THE LEGENDARY PAST WITH LOKI AND WITH US! IN THE WORDS OF NOBLE ODIN -- SO BE IT!

THE END

SEE HOW VERY *SKILLFUL* ULLER IS! HE IS SURE TO DEFEAT THE MORE CLUMSY VOLSAK!

YOU SEEM TO THINK *YOU* KNOW EVERY-THING, THOR! I'LL WAGER A GLODEN GLOBULE THAT *VOLSAK* WILL BE THE VICTOR!

THOR IS *RIGHT!* ULLER *IS* THE MORE SKILLFUL!

BUT, I CAN'T BEAR THE WAY THOR IS SO SELDOM WRONG!

A WORTHY BLOW, ULLER! MY FATHER, NOBLE ODIN, HAS INDEED TRAINED YOU WELL!

SEE, LOKI! ULLER IS BUT SECONDS AWAY FROM VICTORY!

AGAIN THOR HAS BEEN PROVEN RIGHT--WHILE *LOKI* IS WRONG! BUT THERE IS STILL TIME FOR ME TO SAVE THE DAY-- IF I MOVE QUICKLY!

ONE SIMPLE SPELL, TAUGHT TO ME BUT A FEW DAYS AGO BY THE *NORN WITCH WOMEN* MIGHT CHANGE THE TIDE OF BATTLE!

HOW I LONG FOR THE DAY WHEN *I,* TOO, SHALL HAVE THE RIGHT TO BRANDISH A WAR CLUB DURING SUCH A JOUST!

2

SUDDENLY...

I DO NOT UNDERSTAND! MY QUARTER-STAFF SIMPLY *FELL APART!*

IT COULD ONLY HAVE BEEN THE WORK OF A *SPELL!* AND I SEE THE CULPRITS *NOW!*

IT MATTERS NOT! *VOLSAK* IS THE WINNER!

QUICK, THOR! WE MUST FLEE, BEFORE THEY *SEIZE* US!

NEVER! THE SON OF ODIN RUNS FROM *NO ONE!*

IT'S *THOR*-- AND *LOKI!*

GET THEM!

YOU KNOW THE RULES ABOUT INTERFERING WITH A *TOURNAMENT,* LOKI!

WHY DO YOU SPEAK ONLY TO MY *BROTHER?*

WE KNOW THAT *YOU* WOULD NOT HAVE DONE SO BASE A DEED, YOUNG THOR!

3

BUT, I WAS AT THE *SIDE* OF LOKI! IF THERE IS ANY PUNISHMENT TO BE METED OUT, *I* MUST SHARE IT WITH HIM!

YOU ARE *TRULY* THE SON OF *ODIN!* YOUR SOUL IS AS NOBLE AS THE NAME YOU BEAR!

BECAUSE OF YOUR *GALLANTRY,* YOUNG PRINCE, THERE SHALL BE *NO* PUNISHMENT! THE INCIDENT IS *OVER!*

HOW THEY BOW AND SCRAPE BEFORE HIM --GIVING HIM THE DUE THAT SHOULD BE *MINE!* I CANNOT *BEAR* THE SIGHT!

ON BEHALF OF LOKI AND MYSELF, I CRAVE YOUR FORGIVENESS, NOBLE LORDS!

GRANTED, YOUNG NOBLEMAN! YOU AND LOKI ARE FREE TO DEPART!

MARK YE WELL MY WORDS! NO GOOD WILL COME OF THE UN-SCRUPULOUS LOKI!

THOUGH HE BE NOT YET FULL-GROWN, THE SEED OF EVIL HAS ALREADY TAKEN ROOT!

BUT, SEE HOW LIKE A KING THE GOLDEN ONE WALKS! *BY ASGARD,* HE IS DESTINED FOR GREATNESS!!

4

IF THEY WOULD BOW TO *ME* AS THEY DO TO *THOR*, I'D FIND A WAY TO GAIN COMPLETE *CONTROL* OVER THEM! FOR I WAS *BORN* TO BE SERVED--TO GIVE COMMANDS!

IT WAS *FOOLISH* OF YOU TO INTERFERE WITH THE TOURNAMENT, LOKI--BUT, WHAT IS DONE IS DONE!

IT IS TIME FOR OUR HORSEMANSHIP TRAINING NOW!

COME ON, LOKI! I'LL RACE YOU TO THE FOOT OF THE RAINBOW BRIDGE!

NO! WHY *SHOULD* I? YOU HAVE A FASTER STEED!

IT IS NOT ALONE THE *HORSE* THAT MATTERS--BUT THE ONE WHOSE HANDS ARE HOLDING THE REINS!

BLAST HIM!! HE DEFEATS ME AT *EVERYTHING!* SEE HOW HE RIDES--SMILING --A SONG ON HIS LIPS-- FOREVER UNBEATEN!

THERE'S THE BRIDGE AHEAD, LOKI! FASTER! TRY *HARDER!* I'M RACING AWAY FROM YOU!

I *SHALL* TRY HARDER!! I SHALL DEVOTE MY *LIFE* TO GAINING THE MOST *POWER* IN ASGARD! AND, I KNOW THAT SOONER OR LATER, IN ORDER TO ATTAIN MY GOAL, *THOR* MUST BE DESTROYED!!

THE END

AND LOKI'S STILL *AT* IT--OR IS THERE SOMEONE IN MIDGARD WHO HASN'T *NOTICED?* EXCELSIOR!

SUPREMELY CONFIDENT, BECAUSE OF HIS GARGANTUAN SIZE, THE RAMPAGING STORM GIANT HURLS A MONSTROUS BOULDER WITH THE FORCE OF A THUNDERCLAP!

DEATH TO THE PUNY LEGIONS OF ODIN!

BUT, FEARLESSLY WIELDING HIS ENCHANTED HAMMER, THE VALIANT *THOR* SHATTERS GHAN'S CAREENING BOULDER INTO A THOUSAND FRAGMENTS!

FOR ASGARD!

THUS, THE BATTLE BEGINS! BUT, ONE THERE IS WHO HANGS BACK -- OUT OF HARM'S WAY...

LET THE *OTHERS* DO THE FIGHTING! LET *THEM* SUFFER THE INJURIES AND THE PAIN!

THE CUNNING *LOKI* IS FAR TOO CLEVER TO TAKE NEEDLESS CHANCES! I SHALL REMAIN HERE, IN SAFETY -- AND PLAN THE DEFEAT OF MY HATED HALF-BROTHER!

2

THE ENCHANTMENT OF MY FLASHING *SWORD* SHALL UNDO ALL THAT THE THUNDER GOD'S *HAMMER* CAN HOPE TO ACCOMPLISH!

I SHALL CAST A SPELL TO GIVE *GHAN* THE FINAL VICTORY-- AND THUS SHALL I CAUSE THE DOWNFALL OF HE WHOM I SO DESPISE!

BUT, BEFORE LOKI'S EVIL SPELL CAN TAKE EFFECT, THE ARROWS OF THE WARRIORS OF ASGARD CAUSE THE LUMBERING STORM GIANT TO HALT HIS DEVASTATING ATTACK--!

SEE HOW THE VILLAINOUS GHAN FEARS TO ADVANCE ANY FURTHER!

LET YOUR CROSSBOWS SING! HE MUST NOW BE DRIVEN *BACK!*

THEN, SUDDENLY, WITH AN EAR-PIERCING ROAR OF HELPLESS RAGE, THE BRUTAL BEHEMOTH TURNS AND FLEES FROM HIS SMALLER FOES!

HE MUST NOT *ESCAPE* US! PREPARE TO LET LOOSE THE *CATAPULT!*

THE *SLEEP FUMES* WITHIN THIS CONTAINER WILL MAKE HIM LOSE THE WILL TO FIGHT AS SOON AS HE INHALES THEM!

3

RELEASE THE CATAPULT!!

IT IS DONE!

FORWARD, WARRIORS OF ASGARD! WE MUST SEIZE THE GIANT INVADER BEFORE THE FUMES ARE BLOWN AWAY!

BUT, UPON REACHING THE SITE WHERE GHAN SHOULD BE WAITING, THEY FIND...

THE STORM GIANT HAS VANISHED --WITHOUT A TRACE!

THERE IS NO WAY HE COULD HAVE ESCAPED-- EXCEPT THRU THE AID OF A SINISTER MAGIC SPELL!

THERE IS NO SIGN OF HIM! IT IS AS THOUGH HE HAS NEVER EXISTED!

BUT, GHAN POSSESSED NO SUCH MYSTIC POWERS! AND, IF NOT HE, THEN WHO--??

THUS PUZZLED, THE NOBLE THUNDER GOD SCANS THE HORIZON, SEARCHING FOR SOME UNEXPECTED FOE-- BUT, IN VAIN! FOR, NEVER WOULD AN IMMORTAL OF ASGARD SUSPECT THAT ONE OF HIS OWN COULD BE A SCHEMING TRAITOR--!

I'VE DONE IT! I'VE SEIZED VICTORY FROM MY UNWITTING HALF-BROTHER! THIS SHALL BE THE FIRST OF MANY FAILURES FOR THOR!

4

THE TRUSTING FOOLS! THEY *BELIEVED* ME WHEN I SAID I WISHED TO STAY AND SEARCH SOME MORE! *THOR* EVEN PRAISED MY DEVOTION TO DUTY!

AND, AS SOON AS THE VALIANT BAND OF WARRIORS ARE SAFELY OUT OF SIGHT, THE CUNNING GOD OF EVIL MAKES A MYSTIC GESTURE, CAUSING THE HIGH-FLYING BIRD OF PREY TO RETURN TO ITS *NATURAL* FORM...

LET THE GIANT *GHAN* APPEAR ONCE MORE!

LOKI! YOU HAVE SAVED ME FROM THE VENGEANCE OF THOR!

I KNOW NOT WHAT MOTIVES CAUSED YOU TO BETRAY YOUR OWN KIND, BUT THAT IS NO CONCERN OF *MINE!* KNOW YOU, LOKI, THAT *GHAN* IS IN YOUR DEBT!

I SHALL NEVER *FORGET* IT, GIGANTIC ONE --AND NEITHER SHALL *YOU!* THE DAY WILL COME WHEN I ORDER YOU TO *REPAY* THIS DEBT!

THUS, I HAVE MADE MY FIRST ALLIANCE WITH THE FORCES OF EVIL-- WITH ONE OF THOSE WHO WILL COME TO MY AID WHEN I MAKE MY FINAL BID TO OVERTHROW THE RULE OF ODIN, DESTROY THOR, AND SEIZE THE THRONE OF ASGARD.!!

YOU HAVE BEEN PRIVILEGED TO PEER MANY MANY AGES BACK-- BACK INTO THE EARLY HISTORY OF ASGARD, WHEN THE TRUE MENACE OF LOKI WAS JUST BEGINNING TO MAKE ITSELF KNOWN! SEE HOW THE GOD OF EVIL CONTINUES HIS EFFORT TO MUSTER ADDITIONAL ALLIES IN OUR NEXT GREAT ISSUE, AND IN MANY ISSUES TO COME! SEE ALSO WHY *TALES OF ASGARD* HAS WON UNIVERSAL ACCLAIM AS THE MOST ARTISTIC, THE MOST CLASSICAL ENDEAVOR IN THIS, THE MARVEL AGE OF COMICS!

But hold! Before you take your leave of the hallowed realm, one more precious gem of knowledge must I now impart. It occurred to me that the three brief chapters depicting Loki's origin which you have just passionately perused might only serve to whet your appetite for a full-length battle between the sinister sorcerer and the noble Thor. And you know how we try to anticipate your every wish and desire.

Therefore, while issue #115 was still lying open before us, dazzling our eyes and nurturing our senses, we decided to reprint the sixteen-page Thor novelette from that very issue—the tale entitled "The Vengeance of the Thunder God." It even contains a little surprise bonus for you. Not only does it present Loki in all his diabolical dastardliness, but it also features another of the Thunder God's most famous foes, the ever-popular, ever-despicable Absorbing Man, with a fantastic demonstration of his astonishing powers!

I know it must be difficult for you to accept the fact that any book such as this can bestow such beneficence upon its grateful readers. And yet, think of this only as a small token from those who guard the golden gates, from those who serve the eternal realm, for thee—who hast lit the light and kept the faith! Yea verily, thou hast been loyal—thou hast been true—and for thine eyes alone we now presenteth the Mighty Thor, in battle as thou lovest him best. . . .

THE MIGHTY THOR!

"the VENGEANCE of the THUNDER GOD"

THE EVIL *LOKI* HAS CAPTURED JANE FOSTER!! WITH THOSE STAGGERING WORDS RINGING IN HIS EARS, MIGHTY *THOR* ABANDONS HIS EARTHLY BATTLE WITH THE *ABSORBING MAN!** LIKE A LIVING ENGINE OF DESTRUCTION, THE RAGING IMMORTAL RETURNS TO ASGARD, BRAVING THE MENACE OF LOKI'S DEADLY *TRAP....!*

STORY BY:
STAN LEE
THE SAGE OF THE MARVEL AGE!

PENCILING BY:
JACK KIRBY
THE RAGE OF THE MARVEL AGE!

INKING BY:
FRANKIE RAY
FOR HIS WAGE IN THE MARVEL AGE!

LETTERING BY:
ARTIE SIMEK
FROM HIS CAGE IN THE MARVEL AGE!

RESPECTFULLY DEDICATED TO *YOU*, THE GREAT, NEW BREED OF MAGAZINE READER!

*AS PRESENTED IN *THOR #114*...STAN

103

AT *LAST*, DESPISED HALF-BROTHER, YOU HAVE MADE YOUR MOST FATAL BLUNDER! YOU HAVE STUPIDLY CHOSEN TO BATTLE ME ON MY *HOME GROUNDS*! NOW YOU SHALL LEARN THAT *LOKI* IS TRULY YOUR MASTER!

MY ENCHANTED SWORD --- AGAINST YOUR ENCHANTED HAMMER! THOUGH THEIR POWER BE EQUAL, MY CUNNING *BRAIN* GIVES *ME* THE ADVANTAGE!

IT'S LIKE SOME MAD NIGHTMARE!! WHY WOULD THE *THUNDER GOD* RISK EVERYTHING TO RESCUE *ME*!

HOW DID *I* BECOME A PAWN IN THIS BATTLE OF *TITANS*??

YOUR CUNNING SHALL NOT SAVE YOU *NOW*, EVIL ONE! NAUGHT BUT NAKED *POWER* CAN STOP THE FIRST-BORN OF ODIN! *THIS* TIME YOU HAVE SEALED YOUR DOOM!

BAH! YOURS IS THE POWER OF THE BUMBLING OAF!! *MINE* IS THE POWER OF THE MASTER SCHEMER!

AND REMEMBER -- WHILE YOU STILL CAN -- THOUGH OUR *WEAPONS* BE EQUAL, LOKI IS PRINCE OF *SORCERY*!

AND PRINCE OF *BRAGGARTS*, AS WELL! BUT, WE ARE BOTH PLEDGED NEVER TO HARM A MORTAL BEING, AND YOU HAVE *BROKEN* THAT PLEDGE BY CAPTURING THE EARTH GIRL!

FOR *THAT* BETRAYAL, MY HEART CAN HOLD NO FORGIVENESS!

FOOL! I HAVE NOT HARMED HER! SHE WAS MERELY *BAIT*, TO LURE YOU TO ME!

BUT, NEVER AGAIN SHALL YOU USE SUCH BAIT! NEVER AGAIN SHALL AN UNWITTING HUMAN SERVE YOUR EVIL PURPOSE!

AHHH! I *WARNED* YOU OF MY SORCERY! YOUR HAMMER CANNOT SHATTER MY SWORD! I MERELY WILL MY BLADE TO ENTER ANOTHER DIMENSION!!

AND NOW, IT IS *LOKI'S* TURN TO STRIKE --!

2

BUT, WHILE THE AWESOME BATTLE RAGES IN FAR-OFF ASGARD, EVENTS ARE TRANSPIRING ON EARTH WHICH ALSO MERIT OUR SERIOUS ATTENTION...

YOU'RE *HARRIS HOBBS*, THE REPORTER FOR *AFFILIATED PRESS!* WHAT ARE YOU DOING OUT *HERE*, HOBBS?

SAME THING *YOU* ARE! I'M LOOKING FOR THE ESCAPED CONVICT, *CRUSHER CREEL!*

WHAT'S ALL THIS ABOUT PEOPLE CALLING HIM THE *ABSORBING MAN?* WHAT DOES IT MEAN?

UNBELIEVABLE AS IT MAY SOUND, CREEL IS ABLE TO *ABSORB* THE POWER OF ANYTHING NEAR HIM -- HE ABSORBS IT INTO HIS OWN *BODY!* IF HE IS NEAR *IRON*, HIS BODY ITSELF POSSESSES THE POWER OF IRON!

MISTER, YOU SOUND LIKE A *NUT* TO ME!

LOOK-- THERE ARE MY *CREDENTIALS!* I'M NO WILD-EYED FANATIC! I *SAW* CREEL'S BODY CHANGE!

I WAS THERE WHEN HE BATTLED *THOR* HIMSELF! NO MATTER WHAT THOR DID, HE COULDN'T BEAT THE *ABSORBING MAN!* FOR, BY STANDING NEAR THE THUNDER GOD, CREEL BECAME EQUALLY POWERFUL!

EVEN CREEL'S *BALL AND CHAIN* BECAME AS POTENT AS THOR'S OWN *HAMMER!*

EVEN IF YOU *FIND* HIM, I DON'T KNOW HOW YOU CAN *CAPTURE* HIM!!

AND, A FEW MILES TO THE NORTH, HUNGRY AND TIRED, THE *ABSORBING MAN* COMES UPON A LONELY HOUSE, PEACEFULLY NESTLED AMONGST THE WOODED ACRE-AGE OF A WEALTHY SUBURBAN COMMUNITY...

THAT'S WHAT I NEED -- A PLACE TO GET SOME GRUB, AND A BED FOR THE NIGHT!

*B*RAZENLY, THE MERCILESS FUGITIVE MOUNTS THE STEPS, FEARING *NOTHING* WITH HIS NEW-FOUND POWER--!

IF ANYONE'S AT HOME, IT'LL BE JUST TOO BAD --FOR *THEM!*

AND, WITHIN THE LUXURIOUSLY-FURNISHED LIVING ROOM, HE SEES...

IT'S GOOD TO BE HOME, ANN! I HAD A TRYING DAY AT THE BANK TODAY!

YOU JUST SIT DOWN AND READ YOUR PAPER, DEAR! I'LL HAVE DINNER READY BEFORE YOU KNOW IT!

3

ONE BOON, NOBLE FATHER! GRANT ME **48 HOURS** TO BRING THE GIRL TO EARTH, AND FINISH A BATTLE WHICH I HAD BEGUN--THEN SHALL I RETURN TO ASGARD TO ENDURE THE TRIAL OF THE GODS!

DENY HIM, SIRE! HE SEEKS TO **ESCAPE!**

THE THUNDER GOD'S WORD SHALL BE HIS BOND! 48 HOURS-- **SO BE IT!**

THUS, THE IMMORTAL AVENGER RETURNS TO THE PLANET WHICH HAS BECOME HIS OTHER HOME-- CARRYING THE GIRL HE LOVES GENTLY CRADLED WITHIN TWO ARMS--ARMS WHOSE POWER DEFIES DESCRIPTION!

SLEEP, MY BELOVED, FOR YOU ARE SAFE ONCE MORE! NOTHING CAN HARM THEE NOW!

FRAIL MORTAL SENSES WERE NOT MEANT TO COPE WITH THE SIGHTS SHE HAS SEEN, THE THINGS SHE HAS HEARD!

THEREFORE, BY THE POWERS AT MY COMMAND, I GRANT THEE THE GIFT OF-- FORGETFULNESS!

UPON AWAKENING, MY LOVED ONE, YOU SHALL REMEMBER NAUGHT THAT HAS TRANSPIRED!

THEN, SATISFIED THAT JANE FOSTER IS SAFE AND SOUND, THE MIGHTY **THOR** PREPARES ONCE AGAIN TO BATTLE THE UNBEATABLE--!

NO MATTER WHAT THE COST, I MUST AGAIN LOCATE THE **ABSORBING MAN!**

FOR I HAVE PLEDGED MY VERY **LIFE** TO THE DEFENSE OF EARTH!

AND, SO LONG AS THAT DEADLY MENACE EXISTS UNCHECKED, ALL MANKIND IS IN THE GRAVEST DANGER!

6

AND, IN ANOTHER SECTION OF THE STATE...

IF YOU THINK YOU CAN BREAK INTO MY HOUSE AND GET AWAY WITH IT, YOU'VE ANOTHER THINK COMING!

NOW, I'LL GIVE YOU FIVE MINUTES TO GET GOING BEFORE I CALL THE POLICE!

IZZAT SO?

MISTER, IT'S TIME I BEGIN YOUR EDUCATION! YOU GOT A LOT TO LEARN ABOUT CRUSHER CREEL!

MAYBE YOU AINT HEARD ABOUT IT YET, BUT I'M THE GUY WHO JUST FOUGHT THOR TO A STAND-STILL AND MADE 'IM GO RUNNIN' OFF WITH HIS TAIL BETWEEN HIS LEGS!

THAT'S IMPOSSIBLE! YOU MUST BE MAD!

TAKE YOUR HANDS OFF MY HUSBAND, YOU HORRIBLE BRUTE!

NO, ANN-- DON'T!! KEEP OUT OF THIS!!

THAT'S OKAY, MISTER! SHE CAN'T BOTHER THE ABSORBING MAN!

WHA--?!!

NOW DO YA SEE WHY NOTHIN' CAN STOP ME?? I ABSORB THE POWER OF ANYTHING I'M ATTACKED WITH! GLASS, WOOD, STEEL--- EVEN THOR'S HAMMER!

I-I CAN'T BELIEVE IT! IT MUST BE SOME KIND OF--OF TRICK!

BUT-- LOOK AT HIM!! HE-HE'S MADE OF GLASS!

NOT ANY MORE I AINT! I CAN BECOME RAW SILK, JUST BY TOUCHIN' THIS CURTAIN!

JOHN! THIS IS MADNESS! WHAT WILL WE DO? WHERE WILL IT END?

EASY, DEAR! WE'VE GOT TO SEE IT THRU, SOMEHOW!

7

109

111

I'VE GOT TO *TAUNT* HIM, LIKE THOR SAID -- TO GET HIM OUT OF THE HOUSE!

A *PHONY,* AM I ?? YOU'LL *EAT* THOSE WORDS, REPORTER!!

YOU'RE A *PHONY,* CREEL! THAT POWER OF YOURS IS JUST SOME SORT OF *TRICK!* NOBODY'S REALLY SCARED OF YOU!

CRASH!

I *DID* IT! NOW IT'S UP TO *THOR!*

ANYTHING *PHONY* ABOUT SMASHIN' MY WAY RIGHT THRU THE WALL OF A HOUSE?

COPS!! OKAY, IT'S JUST AS *WELL!* I'LL SHOW YA, ONCE AND FOR ALL, THAT *NONE* OF YA CAN STOP ME!

STAY *BACK,* CREEL!! DON'T MAKE US *FIRE!*

WE'RE NOT *FOOLING,* MISTER! THIS BAZOOKA MEANS *BUSINESS!*

NO! HOLD YOUR FIRE! IN THE NAME OF THE *AVENGERS,* I NOW TAKE COMMAND!

THE AVENGERS HAVE A-1 PRIORITY RATINGS! THOR OUT-RANKS US! DON'T FIRE THAT GUN!

CLANNNG!

THE *THUNDER GOD!*

YOU *FOOL!* BY HITTIN' MY BALL AND CHAIN, YOU MADE ME ABSORB THE STRENGTH OF YOUR *HAMMER!*

NO MATTER! THOUGH IT COSTS MY VERY *LIFE,* I MUST FORCE YOU TO DISPLAY THE FULL EXTENT OF YOUR *EVIL POWER!*

NEVER AGAIN SHALL YOU FIND A VICTIM *UNAWARE!*

10

THUS, ONE OF THE MOST INCREDIBLE BATTLES OF ALL TIME BEGINS, AS THE NEARBY LAW OFFICERS WATCH IN STUNNED SILENCE-- REALIZING THAT THE MIGHTY THUNDER GOD HAS UNDER-TAKEN A SEEMINGLY HOPELESS BATTLE IN ORDER TO GAIN TIME FOR THEM-- TIME TO STUDY THE ENEMY-- TIME TO DEVISE A DEFENSE AGAINST-- THE INDEFENSIBLE.!!

HOW CAN I HOPE TO DEFEAT HIM WHEN *MY* STRENGTH BECOMES *HIS* STRENGTH-- *MY* POWER BECOMES *HIS* POWER?!!

I CAN *ABSORB* WHATEVER I'M HIT WITH.!! THE MORE YA USE THAT HAMMER, THE MORE I ABSORB ITS POWER.!!

THE HARDER YOU FIGHT, THE STRONGER MY OWN BALL AND CHAIN BECOMES.!! YOU AINT GOT A *CHANCE*-- *NOBODY'S* GOT A CHANCE.!

THE *ABSORBING MAN* CAN DO ANYTHING-- STOP ANYONE.!! *LOOK!* *LOOK* HOW I BATTER YOU TO YOUR KNEES-- BY ABSORBIN' YOUR *OWN* STRENGTH.!

TRULY, I DARE NOT RESORT TO BRUTE STRENGTH AGAIN.! INSTEAD, BY MY POWER OVER NATURE'S ELEMENTS, LET AN IRRESISTIBLE FORCE OF *HEAT* TRAP HIM WITHIN AN UNBREAKABLE VISE.!

11

113

BUT, ONCE AGAIN THE POWER OF THE **ABSORBING MAN** IS MORE THAN EQUAL TO ANY CHALLENGE! THE FORCE OF HEAT WHICH **THOR** HAS HURLED IS INSTANTLY ABSORBED INTO CREEL'S OWN BODY, AS HIS TRIUMPHANT CRY RINGS OUT LIKE A BANSHEE'S WAIL!

NOW I'M STRONGER THAN **EVER!** I'VE ABSORBED THE POWER OF **HEAT!**

COME **CLOSER**, THUNDER GOD--AND I'LL THROW IT RIGHT **BACK** AT YOU! I CAN **DESTROY** YOU ANY TIME I WANT!

WE CAN'T STAND IDLY BY THIS WAY!! WE'VE GOT TO HELP THOR--SOMEHOW!! ORDER THE MEN TO STAND BY, COLLINS! I'M GOING TO GIVE HIM A BLAST WITH A RIFLE GRENADE!

YES SIR, CAPTAIN!

HEADS UP, THERE! LOOK ALIVE, MEN --DON'T TAKE YOUR EYES OFF CREEL!

A SPLIT-SECOND LATER...

PWANNG!

A **RIFLE-GRENADE!!** HAW!! AS IF **THAT** CAN HURT THE ABSORBING MAN!

THE HEAT OF CREEL'S BODY CAUSED THE MISSILE TO DETONATE ON TARGET! BUT HOW WILL IT AFFECT THE ABSORBING MAN'S **POWER??**

12

UNFLINCHING, THE THUNDER GOD WAITS FOR A REPLY FROM HIS GIGANTIC FOE -- BUT, NONE IS FORTHCOMING! INSTEAD, A MONSTROUS FIST IS RAISED ABOVE THE GOLDEN HEAD -- AND THEN, AT THAT INSTANT, CRUSHER CREEL'S TIME RUNS OUT!

YOU HAVE MADE YOUR CHOICE! NOW, THERE IS NO TURNING BACK! NEVER AGAIN SHALL THE ABSORBING MAN MENACE HUMANITY!

YOUR HAMMER!! IT'S WHIRLIN' SO FAST-- CAN'T SEE IT!! WHA-- WHAT'S HAPPENIN'??

I TRIED TO WARN YOU! BY SPINNING MY EN-CHANTED HAMMER AT CYCLOTRONIC SPEED, I HAVE THE POWER TO TRANSMUTE THE ELEMENTS THEMSELVES!

THUS DO YOU MAKE YOUR NEXT CHANGE-- THE ONE WHICH IS DESTINED TO BE YOUR FINAL CHANGE!

IT WAS LIKE A NUCLEAR EXPLOSION! EVEN THE GROUND IS GLAZED!

BUT, WHAT HAPPENED TO THE ABSORBING MAN?? WHERE DID HE GO??

I SHALL EXPLAIN! BUT YOU MUST PRE-PARE YOURSELF FOR THE UNBELIEVABLE!

KNOWING THAT HE ABSORBED EVERY POWER, EVERY ELEMENT HE CAME IN CONTACT WITH, I REALIZED MY ONLY HOPE OF BEATING HIM WAS TO CREATE ONE SPECIAL ELEMENT!

WHAT ELEMENT WAS THAT?

HELIUM!! HE ABSORBED THE QUALITY OF HELIUM GAS-- THERE! SEE FOR YOURSELF!

14

116

HE HAS BECOME LIGHTER THAN AIR, AND IS SWIFTLY BEING DRAWN INTO THE ATMOSPHERE, AS I PLANNED!

"IN THAT GASEOUS STATE, HE CAN SURVIVE INDEFINITELY! I SHALL ALLOW HIM TO DRIFT THRU SPACE UNTIL THE UNEARTHLY POWER HE POSSESSES IS BUT A USELESS, FORGOTTEN MEMORY! THEN, HE SHALL RETURN TO EARTH, ASSUME HIS RIGHTFUL FORM, AND FINISH OUT THE YEARS OF HIS PRISON SENTENCE! THUS, THE ABSORBING MAN WILL BE HEARD OF NO MORE!"

WHEW! -- I WANTED A SCOOP -- BUT NO NEWS-PAPER WOULD PRINT A YARN LIKE THIS! I'LL HAVE TO SELL IT TO A SCIENCE-FICTION MAG!

IT WOULD REQUIRE THE WISDOM OF ODIN FOR ANY MORTAL TO SAY WHERE SCIENCE ENDS AND FICTION BEGINS!

KNOW YOU, HARRIS HOBBS, THAT YOU HAVE EARNED THE GRATITUDE OF THOR BY YOUR FEARLESS ASSISTANCE!

I USED TO THINK YOU WERE JUST A CON-CEITED, COSTUMED SHOW-OFF! SO, I THANK YOU FOR OPENING MY EYES -- FOR SHOWING ME THE BRAVEST, MOST SELF-SACRIFICING CRUSADER I'VE EVER KNOWN!

THEN, WITH THE REPORTER'S WORDS STILL ECHOING AFTER HIM, THE IMMORTAL AVENGER ONCE AGAIN TAKES TO THE AIR, FOR THERE IS STILL MUCH TO BE DONE IN THE FEW HOURS WHICH YET REMAIN--

MY WORK HERE IS FINISHED--

--BUT MANY ARE THE TASKS WHICH STILL AWAIT ME!

HE'S GONE! NOT MANY GUYS WOULD HAVE LEFT BEFORE EVERYONE HAD A CHANCE TO CONGRAT-ULATE THEM AND TELL THEM HOW GREAT THEY ARE!

THOR IS AN AVENGER! THEY'RE A DIFFERENT BREED, MY FRIEND! PRAISE, AND FAME, MEAN NOTHING TO THEM!

YOU'RE JUST AN AVERAGE BUSINESS EXECUTIVE, JOHN DEAR, BUT YOU PROVED TODAY THAT ANYONE CAN BE AN AVENGER IN SPIRIT, AND IN HEART!

I WAS SO PROUD OF YOUR COURAGE, MY DARLING!

MEANWHILE...

MY TIME IS NEARLY UP! I MUST RETURN TO *ASGARD* WITHIN THE HOUR!

BUT FIRST, I MUST GAZE ONCE MORE UPON MY BELOVED!

FOR, IF I *FAIL* THE TRIAL OF THE GODS, THIS WILL SURELY BE MY *FINAL* LOOK!

THEN, AT THAT VERY MOMENT...

YOUR TIME HAS *COME*, THUNDER GOD! THE TRIAL AWAITS THEE...

I HEAR-- AND I OBEY!

TO *ASGARD*, THEN--!

LOKI WILL HAVE HAD ALL THIS TIME TO *PREPARE* FOR OUR TRIAL--AND YET, I MUST NOT WAVER!

16

WHATEVER MY FATE, I SHALL FACE IT---

--LIKE A *GOD!*

END

THUS, THE GOD OF THUNDER STRIDES UNFLINCHINGLY TOWARDS THE SHIMMERING LIGHTS OF ASGARD, TO FACE THE MYSTERIOUS *TRIAL OF THE GODS!* NEXT ISSUE *YOU* SHALL BE AMONG THE FIRST MORTALS EVER TO BEHOLD THIS STARTLING SPECTACLE! TILL THEN, MAY THE BLESSINGS OF THE GODS BE SHOWERED UPON THEE! SO BE IT!

SCOURGE
OF THE MASTER RACE!

The Red Skull is different. Of all the savagely sinister supervillains in this modestly magnificent little book, he is the only one who had already been created before the Marvel Age of Comics bestowed its blessings upon a thankful human race. Yes, Virginia, there was a Red Skull—even before Stan Lee had joined the fabled Bullpen, although I did play a major part in bringing him back to life in the early sixties. But I can see that this'll be a long and convoluted tale, so settle back comfortably while I try to remember how it happened.

As I mentioned so passionately in *Origins of Marvel Comics,* our little literary and art factory was originally called Timely Comics back in the '30s and '40s. When I first started working at Timely, my two bosses were Joe Simon and Jack Kirby. They were also virtually the entire staff. In fact, one of the reasons they hired me was probably because if you're going to be a boss, you need someone to boss around, right? Right. So enter a wide-eyed teenager named Stan Lee. Two bosses—one "gofer". I kept pretty busy.

Anyway, *Captain America* was the newest and biggest of Timely's titles at that time. I served my apprenticeship proofreading, editing, writing captions for, and finally scripting the early adventures of the ol' masked shield-slinger. And, believe me, it was fun. We didn't let the fact that Cap was a private in Uncle Sam's army inhibit our story lines or curb our imaginations. We found excuses to have him battle creatures in haunted castles, bugeyed monsters in hidden lands, and aliens from God-knows-where, as well as the usual plethora of spies, saboteurs, and the virtually obligatory nefarious Nazi nasties. And, needless to say, since Captain America had been created in the shadow of World War Two, it was from those selfsame Nazis that we

121

obtained our largest, seemingly never-ending supply of vile masters of villainy—the worst of whom was, of course, the rapacious Red Skull.

Now the Red Skull had actually been introduced at the very start of the Captain America series, a short time before I came to work for Timely. Not long afterwards, when I became a script-writer myself, he was one of my very favorite bad guys—the ultimate evil-doer, the villain you loved to hate—and I shared this conviction with most of the Captain America fanatics in the wonderful world of fandom. I've no idea how many stories have been based upon our red-white-and-blue Sentinel of Liberty fighting to foil the mad machinations of the fiend in the crimson skull mask, but it would take an electronic calculator with a brand new battery to accurately tally them all.

However, nothing lasts forever, and in the years following World War Two we reluctantly decided that the interest in Cap's type of superheroic do-gooding was on the wane, so we suspended publication of his title. Naturally, with the cancelling of *Captain America Comics,* the career of the Red Skull likewise came to an ignoble end. But, like old soldiers, comicbook heroes and villains never really seem to die—they just fade away into our muddled little memory banks, as the passing years soon proved.

Some time later, with the advent of Marvel Comics, I decided to inflict Captain America upon the helpless public once again. Jack and I devised a somewhat unusual excuse for his being the same apparent age as he was a few decades ago. You know, we were obsessed with a sense of reality at that time, and had to find a reason for our hero not looking like a middle-aged geezer of fifty. The answer we came up with, as any Marvel scholar knows full well, was to establish the fact that Cap had somehow been "buried" in an iceberg many years ago, and the fact that he had been in a "deep freeze" for that length of time had prevented him from aging! This was all accomplished in an early issue of our *Avengers* magazine, enabling Cap to join the Avengers team and become a part of Marveldom's magnificent menage.

Shortly thereafter, the enthusiastic reception he received prompted me to award our star-spangled hero with his own strip in *Tales of Suspense.* And so, in our sublime unselfishness, we had presented the public with two concurrent Captain America vehicles, just as we've done with Thor and Iron Man and many others from time to time.

122

Well, once C.A. (which is the way we lovingly refer to him amongst ourselves) had been elevated to the richly deserved rank of Marvel stardom, it was only natural that the Red Skull should also reappear. And reappear he did. We found countless reasons and excuses to pit our super-patriot against our super-scoundrel/spy/saboteur in story after story. And then, as it so often happened in my crazy career, I suddenly remembered—the chances were that at least 99% of our enraptured readers hadn't the foggiest idea of who the Red Skull really was, or how he had gotten that way. A grievous situation, and one which we would remedy posthaste!

Luckily, since ol' "King" Kirby had illustrated the very first appearance of the Red Skull lo those many years ago, and since he's gifted with a memory far better than mine (as well as probably having those early copies safely stashed away in a private hiding place), it wasn't hard for him to fill in the gaps of my own remembrances. Gaps, did I say? More like yawning caverns! We talked, we reminisced, we argued—same as always—but finally we came up with a story plot that would present the origin of the Red Skull within the framework of a new and gripping C.A. thriller. How well we succeeded will be for you to judge as you hungrily partake of the literary nourishment that lies ahead.

But, before you get started, I'd like to add another thought or two. I've always felt that one of the Red Skull's main attractions was his name. Names are of incredible importance in comicbooks—as well as in flowers, basketball teams, and puppy dogs. Somehow, I doubt that the Red Skull would have enjoyed the same measure of notoriety, of villaindom success, if his name were the Pink Earlobe—or even the Chartreuse Kneecap. Red seems to go with Skull the way Doctor goes with Doom—or Irving goes with Forbush. Can you imagine thrilling to the exploits of the Sky-Blue Skull, or the Pale-Beige Skull? Perish forbid! Or how about the Red Elbow, or the Red Shinbone? No, it had to be the Red Skull. There was just no other way. That's just what Shakespeare probably said when he muttered "It has to be Romeo and Juliet. Marvin and Juliet just won't make it!"

Another point to ponder is the Skull's appearance. I ask you to note the sophisticated restraint, the subtle underplaying, the lack of ornamentation on his jaunty little jumpsuit. Except for the symbol of the swastika, sewn on his costume for the purpose of preventing our younger readers from mistaking him for a good guy, he could be any airline maintenance man or service station mechanic—until we see his face. And there, students, is where it's at. That's the reason the rest of his garb is so subdued—to call attention to the scarlet skull mask which makes him so unique in the annals of burgeoning bad-hood. Ah yes, my compliments to Jolly Jack for having designed a villain who's a credit to his breed. So long as superhero yarns endure, there'll always be a starring role awaiting bad guys of the caliber of our own gruesomely grotesque, maniacally malevolent, and reprehensibly repulsive Red Skull!

And now, with no further ado (since we've used up our entire supply of ado on the preceding paragraphs), let's turn the page and see what the fuss and furor is all about.

"BEFORE I DISPOSE OF YOU, I SHALL TELL YOU HOW I FIRST BECAME THE RED SKULL -- SECURE IN THE KNOWLEDGE THAT YOUR LIPS WILL NEVER REPEAT MY TALE! MANY YEARS AGO I WAS A NAMELESS ORPHAN, FORCED TO STEAL THE VERY FOOD I NEEDED TO LIVE..."

COME BACK WITH THAT CHICKEN! COME BACK!

YOU WASTE YOUR WORDS! HUNGER LENDS WINGS TO HIS FEET!

"BUT, EVEN AS A THIEF I WAS NOT SUCCESSFUL! I WAS TOO SMALL, TOO WEAK -- I WAS AN EASY PREY FOR THOSE WHO WERE BIGGER!"

IT WAS NICE OF HIM TO BRING US A CHICKEN! BUT, IT IS NOT LARGE ENOUGH!

NEXT TIME HE WILL BRING A BETTER ONE!

"AS I GREW OLDER, MOST OF MY TIME WAS SPENT IN JAIL -- FOR EVERY CRIME FROM VAGRANCY TO THEFT!"

YOU AGAIN?!!

CAN WE NOT GET RID OF YOU?!!

"BUT, WHEN THEY DID GET RID OF ME, I WAS NO BETTER OFF! I SLEPT IN BARNS, STABLES, ANYWHERE I COULD LIE DOWN WITHOUT BEING CHASED AWAY!"

"AND, ON THE RARE OCCASIONS WHEN I FOUND EMPLOYMENT, IT WAS ALWAYS THE MOST MENIAL, THE MOST THANK-LESS OF JOBS..."

YOU! LOOK ALIVE THERE! KEEP SWEEPING, OR GET OUT!

LOTS OF PEOPLE HAD TOUGH LIVES! MY EARLY YEARS WERE NO BED OF ROSES, EITHER! BUT I DON'T WASTE TIME TELLING SOB STORIES!

YOU FORGET YOUR-SELF!! MEN HAVE DIED FOR SPEAKING SO FLIPPANTLY TO ME!

HOWEVER, I AM IN A MERCIFUL MOOD! I SHALL CONTENT MYSELF WITH MERELY A MILD REBUFF -- SUCH AS THIS!

UNNNHHH--!

3

YOU'LL LIVE TO *REGRET* THAT, SKULL!!

YOU ARE *WRONG!* MY DAYS OF REGRETTING ARE *OVER!* TODAY, I AM *SUPREME!* LESSER MEN *COWER* BEFORE ME!

I *WARN* YOU NOW-- DO NOT INTERRUPT MY NARRATIVE AGAIN! IF YOU *DO*, I'LL BE FORCED TO USE *THIS* ON YOU!

AND I WOULD NOT *WANT* TO DO THAT! IT IS TOO SWIFT-- TOO *EASY* A FATE FOR YOU!

"MY LIFE *CHANGED* WHEN THE *NAZIS* CAME TO POWER! I REMEMBER THAT FATEFUL DAY WHEN *ADOLF HITLER* FIRST CAME TO TOWN! HIS STORM TROOPERS WERE OUT IN FORCE, ROUNDING UP ALL UNDESIRABLES FOR HIS PROTECTION...."

YOU ARE NOT A TRUE *ARYAN!* COME WITH *ME!!*

GOOD! GOOD! STRIKE FOR DER *FUEHRER!*

ACHTUNG! CLEAR THE STREETS! THE PROCESSION IS ABOUT TO BEGIN! DER *FUEHRER* HIMSELF IS COMING!

"I WAS WORKING AS A BELLBOY IN THE HOTEL THAT DAY! I REMEMBER WATCHING FROM THE WINDOW-- SEEING THEM TURN OUT BY THE *THOUSANDS* TO WELCOME ADOLF HITLER, THEIR *FUEHRER!*"

HE IS MY EXACT *OPPOSITE!* HE HAS *POWER*--AND I AM *NOTHING!*

"THEN, LATER THAT NIGHT, I BROUGHT REFRESHMENTS TO HITLER'S ROOM--"

I'M ACTUALLY GOING TO *SEE* HIM--UP CLOSE!

4

"AS I ENTERED, THE FUEHRER WAS BERATING HIS GESTAPO CHIEF FOR LETTING A SPY ESCAPE....!"

YOU HAVE FAILED YOUR *FUEHRER!!* WHEN YOU FAIL *ME*, YOU FAIL *GERMANY!!*

BUT, MEIN FUEHRER--IT WAS NOT MY FAULT! I DID MY *BEST!*

SO! *FAILURE* IS YOUR *BEST??* YOU INCOMPETENT FOOL! YOU *BUNGLER!*

WHY HAVE I NO ONE TO TURN TO?? NONE TO *DEPEND* ON?? MUST I CREATE MY *OWN* RACE OF PERFECT ARYANS?? I COULD TEACH THAT *BELL-BOY* TO DO A BETTER JOB THAN *YOU!!*

"AND THEN, IN THAT MOMENT OF SUPREME DESTINY, HE TURNED TO-- *ME!*"

YOU! YOU CRINGING, TREMBLING, SUBSERVIENT *NOBODY!!* YOU ARE LESS THAN *NOTHING* TO ME! BUT I AM YOUR *LEADER!*-- YOUR *FUEHRER!* I AM *HITLER!*

THE WAY YOU *LOOK* AT ME! THE ENVY, THE JEALOUSY IN YOUR EYES! THE SHEER, BLAZING *HATRED!* I *KNOW* THOSE EMOTIONS! YOU *TOO* HATE ALL MANKIND!!

WHAT AN *INSPIRATION* THIS GIVES ME! *YOU* SHALL BE MY GREATEST ACHIEVEMENT! I SHALL MAKE A *PERFECT NAZI* OF YOU! YOU WILL SERVE ME-- YOU WILL BE MY RIGHT ARM! YOU WILL NEVER FAIL ME!

"I WAS GIVEN THE UNIFORM OF A STORM TROOPER! I WAS DRILLED, TRAINED, TAUGHT, DAY AND NIGHT! BUT, ONE DAY, *HITLER* ENTERED--!"

MEIN FUEHRER--!

STOP! DO YOU *HEAR* ME?? *STOP,* I SAY!!

WHAT ARE YOU *DOING* TO HIM?? I DO NOT WANT HIM TO BECOME ANOTHER MERE STORM TROOPER! I WANT HIM TO BE *EVIL PERSONIFIED!*

FOR THIS MOMENT ON, I *PERSONALLY* WILL SUPERVISE HIS TRAINING!!

5

"HITLER SUDDENLY LEFT, RETURNING MINUTES LATER WITH A STRANGE BOX..."

HERE! OPEN THIS BOX! THERE IS A UNIFORM INSIDE! YOU WILL WEAR IT!

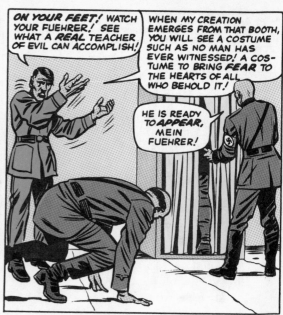

ON YOUR FEET! WATCH YOUR FUEHRER! SEE WHAT A REAL TEACHER OF EVIL CAN ACCOMPLISH!

WHEN MY CREATION EMERGES FROM THAT BOOTH, YOU WILL SEE A COSTUME SUCH AS NO MAN HAS EVER WITNESSED! A COSTUME TO BRING FEAR TO THE HEARTS OF ALL WHO BEHOLD IT!

HE IS READY TO APPEAR, MEIN FUEHRER!

PERFECT!! A TRIBUTE TO MY OWN EVIL GENIUS! HENCEFORTH, YOU SHALL BE KNOWN AS THE RED SKULL-- ANSWERABLE ONLY TO ME!

THAT MASK! SO LIFELIKE-- SO REAL--!!

ALL YOUR LIFE, YOU HAVE NURTURED HATRED WITHIN YOUR BOSOM, AND NOW YOU HAVE POWER TO GO WITH THAT HATRED!

BUT, IT IS TIME FOR YOUR FIRST TEST! I MUST SEE HOW WILLINGLY, HOW COMPLETELY YOU WILL SERVE ME!

THE ONE WHO WAS YOUR INSTRUCTOR HAS FAILED! THERE IS NO ROOM FOR FAILURE IN MY THIRD REICH! SEIZE A GUN!

AND NOW, SHOW HOW YOU TREAT ANY WHO MIGHT BE RASH ENOUGH TO INCUR MY DISPLEASURE!

NO, MEIN FUEHRER --NO!!

YOU BLASTED EVERY BUTTON OFF HIS JACKET!! BUT-- WHY DID YOU LET HIM LIVE??

DEAD, HE IS OF NO FURTHER USE TO YOU!

BUT, ALIVE-- AND FILLED WITH FEAR-- HE IS ANOTHER SLAVE FOR YOU-- HE WILL OBEY YOUR EVERY WHIM!

6

AND NOW, IF I MAY FINISH MY NARRATIVE WITHOUT ANY FURTHER INTERRUPTION!

LET US AGAIN RETURN TO THE EARLY DAYS OF THE WAR--!

"AND, WHAT GLORIOUS DAYS THEY WERE! WHENEVER A CITY WAS LEVELLED, A TOWN WAS SACKED, THE *RED SKULL* WAS THERE!"

"WHENEVER THERE WAS INJUSTICE, TYRANNY, RUTHLESSNESS, THE *RED SKULL* WAS THERE, LEADING THE ATTACK UPON THE WEAK AND THE HELPLESS!"

KEEP FIRING! LET THE WORLD KNOW THAT THE RED SKULL STOPS AT *NOTHING!*

"YES, I SERVED THE FUEHRER WELL -- IN MY OWN FASHION!"

NO, *NO!* YOU CANNOT TAKE MY SON! HE HAS DONE NOTHING! HE IS LOYAL TO THE FUEHRER!

BAH! IT IS HIS LOYALTY TO *ME* THAT COUNTS!! TAKE HIM *AWAY!*

"THANKS TO MY CLEVERNESS, MANY OF HITLER'S MOST TRUSTED ADVISERS BEGAN TO MYSTERIOUSLY *VANISH--!*"

8

DAY BY DAY MY POWER GREW, UNTIL I WAS SECOND ONLY TO HITLER HIMSELF IN SUPREME AUTHORITY! AT MY COMMAND, CITIES WOULD FALL, ARMIES WOULD BE DESTROYED!

"I ORGANIZED AN ENTIRE NEW GROUP OF NAVAL WOLF PACKS, TO DESTROY ENEMY SHIPPING THRUOUT THE WORLD! IT WAS SUCH A UNIT THAT SUNK YOUR OWN CONVOY, ENABLING ME TO CAPTURE YOU!"

BRING ANY SURVIVORS DIRECTLY TO ME FOR QUESTIONING! IF ANY ESCAPE, YOU DIE!

BUT, YOU SEEM TO GROW RESTLESS! CAN IT BE THAT MY LITTLE TALE HAS BORED YOU? PERHAPS I SHOULD TRY TO REVIVE YOUR INTEREST AGAIN--!

YOU'RE A FOOL, NAZI! GLOATING OVER A HELPLESS PRISONER IS A SIGN OF WEAKNESS, NOT STRENGTH!

YOU'VE MADE YOUR POINT, SKULL! I'VE HEARD THAT EVEN HITLER FEARS YOU! EVEN HE CAN NO LONGER CONTROL YOU-- FOR YOU'VE GROWN TOO POWERFUL!

BUT I'M NOT HITLER! I'M AN AMERICAN--

AND MY BREED JUST DOESN'T SCARE EASILY!

BRAVE WORDS, CAPTAIN AMERICA! TOO BAD YOU HAVE NOT THE STRENGTH TO BACK THEM UP!

WHA-WHAT'S HAPPENING TO ME?? MY LEGS WON'T SUPPORT ME--! THE ROOM IS SPINNING--!

9

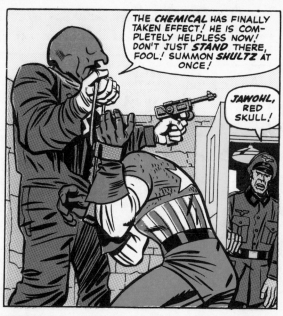

THE *CHEMICAL* HAS FINALLY TAKEN EFFECT! HE IS COMPLETELY HELPLESS NOW! DON'T JUST *STAND* THERE, FOOL! SUMMON *SHULTZ* AT ONCE!

JAWOHL, RED SKULL!

AND SO...

PERFECT! THE POTION WE ADMINISTERED HAS WORKED IN EXACTLY THE TIME I PREDICTED!

AND HE NEVER SUSPECTED A THING!

MY CHEMICAL HAS WIPED HIS MIND CLEAN! IT IS NOW AN EMPTY SLATE, FOR YOU TO WRITE WHATEVER YOU DESIRE UPON IT!

WHEN HE AWAKENS, YOU WILL BE HIS *MASTER!* HE WILL OBEY YOU BLINDLY!

IF ALL GOES AS YOU SAY, I SHALL REWARD YOU BEYOND YOUR FONDEST DREAMS! IF NOT, YOU DIE BEFORE NIGHTFALL!

AND NOW, *AWAKE!* ON YOUR FEET, SOLDIER OF THE THIRD REICH!!

THE TIME HAS COME FOR YOU TO CARRY OUT A *MISSION* FOR ME!

I-- AM-- READY--!

PROVE IT-- BY RETURNING MY SALUTE!! AHHH, THAT IS MORE LIKE IT!

MAY THE POWER OF THE THIRD REICH LAST A THOUSAND YEARS!

THERE IS A *TARGET* TO BE DESTROYED, AND *YOU* MUST BE THE AGENT OF THAT DESTRUCTION!

NAME THE TARGET! I SHALL ATTACK IT AT ONCE!

IT IS *ONE MAN!* THE SUPREME COMMANDER OF THE ALLIED ARMIES!!

THIS IS ONLY THE *BEGINNING!* NEXT CHAPTER, THE PACE BECOMES EVEN FASTER AS THE SUSPENSE GROWS MORE UNBEARABLE! *BE* HERE! WE'LL *PROVE* WHAT WE SAY!

10

134

CAPTAIN AMERICA

LEST TYRANNY TRIUMPH!

HAVING BEEN DRUGGED BY THE VILLAINOUS *RED SKULL*, AMERICA'S MOST GALLANT HERO SUDDENLY BECOMES FREEDOM'S GREATEST *THREAT* AS HE PREPARES TO ATTACK THE ALLIES' TOP MILITARY LEADER!

MIT *CAPTAIN AMERICA* FIGHTING AT OUR SIDE, VE CANNOT *FAIL!*

EFFEN MITOUT FIREARMS, HE ISS DER MOST DEADLY FIGHTING MACHINE VE HAFF EFFER VITNESSED!

STORY AND ART BY: STAN LEE *and* JACK KIRBY

INKING: FRANK RAY

LETTERING: ARTIE SIMEK

AS THE TORTUROUS SESSION CONTINUES, EVERY NEW OBSTACLE TO APPEAR IS FAR MORE DANGEROUS AND DEADLY THAN THE LAST ONE....!

--AND EACH IS OVERCOME WITH THE SPEED AND INGENUITY WHICH HAVE MADE THE NAME *CAPTAIN AMERICA* A VERITABLE LIVING LEGEND!

FINALLY, AFTER EVERY TEST HAS BEEN MET AND CONQUERED...!

ACHTUNG! DER SESSION ISS *ENDED!* DER *RED SKULL* HAS COME!

AND HOW IS OUR NEWEST *RECRUIT* TODAY? SHOW ME YOUR *LOYALTY,* CAPTAIN AMERICA!

HEIL, RED SKULL!

GOOD! GOOD! YOU LEARN YOUR LESSONS WELL!

AND NOW, THE *FINAL* TEST-- TO SEE IF YOUR CONDITIONING HAS MADE YOU READY TO COMMIT THE SUPREME ACT OF DEVOTION TO ME!

TAKE THIS *LUGER!*

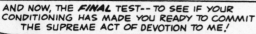

ON THAT SWINGING PENDULUM IS A PHOTOGRAPH OF AMERICA'S TOP MILITARY COMMANDER! HE IS MY ENEMY! *SHOOT HIM!*

2

PERFECT! BULL'S EYE! YOU DID IT WITHOUT FLINCHING -- WITHOUT HESITATION!

NOW, YOU ARE READY FOR THE *REAL THING!*

KRAK!

MEANWHILE, CAP'S TEEN-AGE PARTNER, BUCKY BARNES, WHO HAD BEEN CAPTURED EARLIER, IS LED BEFORE A *FIRING SQUAD* WITH A HANDFUL OF OTHER POLITICAL PRISONERS....!

HAH! IT ISS NOT OFTEN VE HAFF A CHANCE TO SHOOT SOMEVON IN COSTUME!

UP AGAINST DOT VALL! ALL OF YOU! SCHNELL!

SO! VE VILL SEE IF DER YOUTHFUL PARTNER OF *CAPTAIN AMERICA* KNOWS HOW TO *DIE* AS VELL AS HOW TO *FIGHT!*

IF HE EXPECTS ME TO BREAK DOWN AND *BEG,* HE'S GONNA BE ONE DISAPPOINTED KRAUT!

UND NOW, VE *BEGIN!* ACHTUNG!! READY! AIM! UND---

FIRE!

CLICK! CLICK! CLICK!

NAWW! DID YOU THINK IT VOULD BE SO *EASY??* NEIN! VE JUST HAD A *JOKE* MIT YOU!

DIS VAY, VE SHALL *BREAK* YOUR VILL, SOONER OR LATER! YOU VILL NEFFER KNOW VHEN OUR GUNS DO *NOT* CONTAIN BLANKS! DER SUSPENSE VILL MAKE YOU *CRACK!*

3

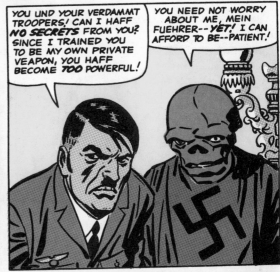

BUT, BEHIND A NEARBY CURTAIN, *OTHER* EARS WERE LISTENING-- AND THEN--

THIS IS THE ONE! HE'S JUST ABOUT MY SIZE!

SORRY, CHUM! YOU'RE GONNA BE SITTIN' THIS MISSION OUT!

ACHTUNG!! *FALL IN!!* IT ISS TIME TO ASSEMBLE AT DER AIRPORT!

VAIT! SOMEVON ISS *MISSING!!* IT ISS *SHULTZ!* VHERE *ISS* DOT UNDERSIZED DUMMKOPF??

HE VAS HERE A *MINUTE* AGO.!!

AHH! DERE HE ISS! ALL RIGHT, *FALL IN!!* VE HAFF NO MORE TIME TO VASTE! EVERY SECOND *COUNTS* NOW.!

MINUTES LATER, AFTER THE COMMANDO-TYPE SQUAD HAS ENTERED THE HEAVILY-ARMED TRANSPORT...

EVERYTHING ISS *READY*, HERR RED SHKULL!

YOU HAVE YOUR ORDERS, CAPTAIN AMERICA! NOW *GO!*

--AND REMEMBER-- YOU MUST NOT FAIL!

IT'S *HIM!!* IT'S *CAP!* BUT-- HE DOESN'T *KNOW* ME! HE'S LOOKING RIGHT *THRU* ME!

SOMETHING'S *HAPPENED* TO HIM! HE'S LIKE A GUY IN A *DAZE*-- LIKE HE'S *HYPNOTIZED!*

7

WITHIN MINUTES, THE DEAFENING SCREETCH OF COUNTLESS AIR RAID SIRENS ALERTS THE BATTERED, BOMBED-OUT, BLEEDING, BUT STILL UNBOWED CITY OF COURAGE, AS *LONDON* KEEPS THE VIGIL--!

IT'S ANOTHER JERRY RAID!

I THOUGHT I SAW FIGURES-- JUMPING--BUT, THE FLARES BLINDED ME!

WHILE SILENTLY, UNDER COVER OF DARKNESS, WITH JET BLACK 'CHUTES, THE SMALL KILLER SQUAD DRIFTS TO EARTH....!

SKILLFULLY LANDING AT A LONELY, PREARRANGED SPOT, THEY ARE QUICKLY MET BY A CIVILIAN-GARBED NAZI AGENT, AND THEN...

QUICKLY! IN HERE! THIS IS THE BUILDING!

THE GENERAL IS IN HIS STUDY! YOU MUST MOVE *FAST!* HE IS SCHEDULED TO LEAVE WITHIN FIVE MINUTES!

DOT ISS ALL DER TIME VE SHALL *NEED!* COME!

NOW I SEE THE WHOLE PLAN! THEY'RE PLANNING TO MURDER AN ALLIED GENERAL! THEY WANT THE WORLD TO KNOW THAT *CAP* DID THE DEED! IT'LL BE THEIR GREATEST PROPAGANDA VICTORY!

YOU ROTTEN *TRAITOR!* I'LL STOP YA *SOMEHOW!*

SHULTZ HASS GONE *MAD!* GRAB HIM!

LOOK! IT *ISN'T* SHULTZ! IT ISS AN *IMPOSTER!*

CAP! CAP! DON'T *DO* IT! STOP 'EM! YOU'VE *GOT* TO STOP 'EM!

8

THEN, AS THE LAST OF THE CAPTIVES ARE LED AWAY...

CAPTAIN AMERICA, I BELIEVE THAT SOME *EXPLANATIONS* ARE IN ORDER!

YES, SIR! THE ABORTIVE ASSASSINATION ATTEMPT WAS ENGINEERED BY HITLER'S MASTER PLANNER, THE *RED SKULL!*

FINALLY, AS CAP'S STORY REACHES ITS CONCLUSION...

OUR NATION OWES YOU A GREAT DEBT, GENTLEMEN... AS DO *I*, PERSONALLY!

NOT AT ALL, SIR! WE *EACH* SERVE FREEDOM IN OUR OWN WAY... AND LIBERTY IS ITS OWN REWARD!

PERSONALLY, I *LIKE* THE IDEA OF A BIG-SHOT GENERAL BEIN' GRATEFUL TO ME!

MEANWHILE, DIRECTLY ACROSS THE ENGLISH CHANNEL, WE FIND...

THE MISSION HAS *FAILED*, HERR RED SKULL! CAPTAIN AMERICA WAS ABLE TO...

SILENCE! DETAILS *BORE* ME!! I HAVE NO TIME TO BROOD OVER FAILURE!

BESIDES, I HAVE *ANOTHER* MISSION PLANNED... WITH AN EVEN *GREATER* PRIZE AT STAKE!

WITHIN 24 HOURS, MY AGENTS WILL STEAL THE ALLIES' MOST POWERFUL NEW WEAPON, AS THEY ATTACK... *PROJECT VANISH!*

PROJECT VANISH??

YOU DIMWITTED INCOMPETENT! HAVE YOU NOT HEARD OF THE NEW WEAPON WHICH IS HIDDEN IN THE NORTH OF ENGLAND?? THE WEAPON WHICH WILL WIN THE WAR FOR *US!!*

AT THIS VERY MOMENT, THE SPECIAL AGENT WHOM I'VE PLANTED IN THE ALLIED PRISONER-OF-WAR COMPOUND IS GETTING READY TO MAKE HIS MOVE!

"...AND, WHEN HE *DOES*, PROJECT VANISH SHALL BE STOLEN RIGHT FROM UNDER THE BRITISHERS' NOSES AS I CELEBRATE MY GREATEST *TRIUMPH!*"

THE SUN IS SETTING! I MUST PUT THE RED SKULL'S PLAN INTO OPERATION, NOW!

3.

WOLFGANG! I HAVE CHOSEN *YOU!* YOU MUST TRY TO *ESCAPE* NOW!

NO! NO! DON'T MAKE ME DO IT! I DON'T *WANT* TO! THEY'LL *SHOOT* ME!

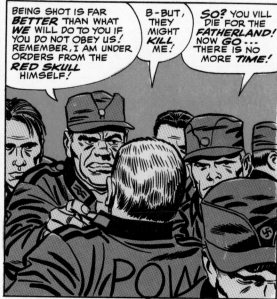

BEING SHOT IS FAR *BETTER* THAN WHAT *WE* WILL DO TO YOU IF YOU DO NOT OBEY US! REMEMBER, I AM UNDER ORDERS FROM THE *RED SKULL* HIMSELF!

B-BUT, THEY MIGHT *KILL* ME!

SO? YOU VILL DIE FOR THE *FATHERLAND!* NOW GO... THERE IS NO MORE *TIME!*

I HAVE NO OTHER *CHOICE!* IF I REFUSE, *THEY* WILL MURDER ME BEFORE THE SUN RISES! AT LEAST THE AMERICAN GUARDS MAY BE MORE MERCIFUL!

SO FAR, SO GOOD! HE IS *CERTAIN* TO BE SHOT...AND THEN *I* WILL REPLACE HIM ON THE SUPPLY TRUCK!

A PRISONER... TRYING TO ESCAPE... RIGHT PAST OUR SENTRY POST! HE MUST BE *MAD!*

HALT! HALT!... OR I'LL *FIRE!*

I MUST KEEP RUNNING..OR THE *OTHERS* WILL KILL ME!

CAN'T LET HIM *ESCAPE*... BUT THERE'S NO NEED TO TAKE HIS LIFE! I'LL GET HIM IN THE *LEG!*

KRAK!

UHHH!

THUS, EARLY THE NEXT MORNING, PRIVATE STEVE ROGERS AND COMPANY MASCOT BUCKY BARNES GUARD THE NEW PRISONER WHO IS REPLACING THE WOUNDED WOLFGANG...

WHAT A JOB FOR A BATTLE-TRAINED COMBAT MAN... GUARDING A HELPLESS PRISONER!

THAT NEW KRAUT IS SOME MEAN-LOOKING EGG! HASN'T SAID A WORD ALL MORNING!

4.

148

150

BUT, AGAIN THE NAZI AGENT HAS MANAGED TO MAINTAIN HIS GRIP UPON THE DREAD RAY MACHINE, AND AS THE SHOCK WAVE PASSES...

IF I AM TO BE DEFEATED, I'LL TAKE THE ENTIRE VERDAMMTE TANK FORCE *WITH* ME!

I'VE GOT TO REACH HIM... I'VE *GOT* TO..!

BUT...CAN'T *MOVE!* MY LEGS...NUMB... I-I'M *HELPLESS!!!*

JUMP!! THE TANK IS BEGINNIN' TO *FADE AWAY!!*

IT'S *PROJECT VANISH!!* SOMEONE'S GOTTEN CONTROL OF THE RAY GUN!!

WOW! LOOK AT *THAT!!* THE WHOLE FRONT OF THE TIN CAN IS *GONE...* LIKE IT JUST *MELTED INTO NOTHINGNESS!*

CLEAR THE AREA!! CONDITION *RED!!* ON THE DOUBLE!! *CLEAR THE AREA!!*

HAH! THEY'RE FLEEING! THAT LEAVES ME ALONE WITH THE RAY! SOON IT WILL BE IN THE HANDS OF THE *NAZIS!*

THEN GO!..*TAKE* IT! JUST DON'T FIRE IT AT ANYONE ELSE! DON'T SET IT TO *FULL INTENSITY!*

FOOL! I WOULDN'T HAVE THOUGHT OF IT, BUT *NOW...* I'LL WIPE OUT *EVERYONE* WITH ONE MORE BLAST..AT *FULL INTENSITY!*

BUT, AS THE FATEFUL TRIGGER IS SQUEEZED...

ARRHHH!

THAT *BLAST!* CAP WAS IN THERE! I-I'VE GOTTA *FIND* HIM!!

FAN OUT, MEN! SHOOT ANYTHING THAT *MOVES!*

THERE HE *IS!* HE'S STILL *ALIVE!* I'VE GOT TO *HELP* HIM!

SILENTLY, THE VALIANT YOUTH DRAGS HIS INJURED PARTNER BEHIND A CONCEALING BOULDER, AS THE OTHER G.I.S GATHER AROUND THE UNCONSCIOUS NAZI ...

I'LL BE ALL RIGHT, BUCKY! QUICK.. BRING MY UNIFORM BEFORE THEY FIND ME!

BUT HOW'D YOU *DO* IT, CAP? HOW'D YOU *BEAT* HIM?

I TRICKED HIM INTO PRESSING THE *FULL INTENSITY* CONTROL! I *KNEW* THE RAY WASN'T YET PERFECTED!

WATCH IT, SGT. DUFFY! WE GOTTA TAKE THIS JERRY BACK TO BASE HOSPITAL!

HE'S ALL YOURS, SOLDIER! I'M LOOKIN' FOR THAT GOLDBRICKIN' YARD-BIRD, *STEVE ROGERS!*

HAVEN'T SEEN 'IM, SARGE!

THAT'S THE END OF PROJECT VANISH! THE RAY WAS TOO UNSTABLE! THEY'LL NEVER WORK ON IT AGAIN!

MEDIC! OVER HERE, FELLA! I FOUND STEVE ROGERS!

OKAY, BARNES! DUFFY WAS JUST LOOKIN' FOR 'IM, TOO!

WHATJA SAY? DID I HEAR SOME-ONE MENTION *ROGERS?* WHERE IS HE? WHERE *IS* HE?

DON'T WORRY, SARGE! HE'LL BE OKAY!

THAT MEANS HE'LL BE BACK IN *MY PLATOON* AGAIN! AND *YOU* TELL ME NOT TO *WORRY!*

AWRIGHT, MEDIC! SEE THAT YA PATCH 'IM UP REAL PRETTY!

WE DON'T WANT 'EM TO POST-PONE THE *WAR* BECAUSE ROGERS AIN'T UP TO SNUFF!

BUT THE WAR, ALAS, WAS *NOT* POSTPONED -- AND TODAY THERE IS *NO* PVT. ROGERS! BUT THERE IS STILL *CAPTAIN AMERICA* -- SPEARHEAD OF THE MIGHTY *AVENGERS!*

10

THE FIEND
FLIES BY NIGHT!

Well, there are villains and there are villains. Which is not necessarily to be construed as a typical example of the far-reaching height of Stan Lee's profundity. But of all the villains who have ever blemished the fair name of valor, none has been more memorable or more many-faceted than the highly complex character known as The Green Goblin.

Gobby is truly the only supervillain who is also a good guy when he's not breaking up Spidey's act. He's also the only supervillain who sometimes doesn't even know who he is in his other identity. And he is for sure the only supervillain who also happens to be the doting father of our hero's best friend. If that doesn't qualify him for a permanent place in The Bad Guys' Hall of Fame, then try this on for size: he's certainly the only comicbook menace to finally reach that old rascals' resting place in the sky and then be replaced by his closest living relative back here on earth! But that happens much later in the series so, lucky for both of us, we won't have to deal with it in this particular book.

Y'know, it's a shame that no one suspected how popular Marvel would become 'way back there in the early days of our collective adolescence. If I had known that there would one day be a series of books such as this which would trace the development of our various creations, I assure you we'd have organized things differently, beginning every series with a neat and handy origin story, readily available for future reprinting, and needing little or no complicated explanation from this weary and woebegone friendly neighborhood scripter.

However, not being aware that I'd one day be accountable for this whole mixed-up megillah, I just let things happen in the natural course of events while your busy little Bullpen and I merrily floated along with the tide. What I'm trying to say is, when you're in the comicbook biz, grinding out as many as two, three, four or more complete issues a week, you simply take your characters as you invent them and employ them wherever you feel they'll fit the best. Hence, a new character will suddenly pop up in any given story, all set to challenge the hero, fullblown and itching for a fight, with none of us realizing that we'll be wishing, in years to come, that we had provided an origin tale at the start, which would make life a zillion times easier for me at a time like this. But, since it didn't work that way, here we are again trying once more to make a modicum of sense out of all this chronological confusion.

In the case of the Green Goblin, I originally introduced him in one of the earliest *Spider-Man* comics, where he was first illustrated—and masterfully delineated—by Steve Ditko. We expected him to be popular with our readers, but the avalanche of mail and the extent of the enthusiasm he engendered was almost indescribable. We knew at once that The Green Goblin was fated to become one of Marvel's most important supervillains. And we treated him accordingly.

The Goblin appeared time after time to threaten poor Spidey, and often the battle would continue for two or three issues. Gobby proved to be far too interesting for us ever to dispose of in only one story. And, in case I haven't mentioned this before, this would be as good a time as any to tell you that there's something almost scary about writing our little sagas—something that borders on the supernatural. No matter how we may try to control their actions, it sometimes seems as if our heroes and villains have lives of their own, lives that follow their own courses, despite all our efforts to alter them. I wish I could tell you how many times John Romita and I tried to present a Green Goblin episode in a given *Spider-Man* yarn in a certain way, only to find that we simply couldn't do it that way—it was as though the characters themselves were forcing us to change the plot, to structure the pictures and the dialogue in another way, a way that was more in keeping with the lives they led . . . or should have led . . . or wanted to lead! Nope, you'll never convince me that a fictional character is nothing more than the product of his creator's brain. Once he's been brought to life on the printed page he assumes another dimension, another quality that no one yet has put a name to, but a quality that definitely exists. Maybe we'll save this subject for another book; it's too metaphysical to get into right now. So, back to the Goblin.

Despite the years that Steve and I spent collaborating on the web-slinger's adventures, we never really got around to presenting an origin story for the Green Goblin. Later, after Steve had left the Bullpen and one of Marvel's all-time ace illustrators, Jazzy Johnny Romita, replaced him on the strip, bringing a magnificent new style and new gestalt to our little cast of characters, we decided we'd integrate an origin sequence within the story that was to mark "finis" to the Goblin's exploits. I felt it would be highly dramatic to finally show what made the Goblin the way he was in the selfsame story that was to mark the end of his career. However, as we just discussed, it didn't quite work out that way. Oh, we did our origin sequence all right—as you will shortly see—but as for the Goblin himself, he just wouldn't stay dead. Still, since that's no concern to us now, let's get back to Gobby himself.

If it sounds to you as though we're in a rut, what with The Green Goblin, The Red Skull, The Silver Surfer, and the countless others who seem to have a color for a first name, blame it on my burning desire for visual imagery. I love a name that conjures up an instant image, a name that plants a picture in your mind the minute you hear it. Somehow I feel that the name "Green Goblin" doesn't leave much doubt as to what type of guy you're about to see.

The Goblin has always been a favorite of mine because he's so extremely offbeat. In the beginning, we didn't know who he'd turn out to be when he was finally unmasked. But, instead of making him some ordinary crook or scheming criminal mastermind, I was intrigued with the notion of his being an everyday "good guy"; and, even better than that, someone very close to Peter Parker's best friend. It suited my own sense of dramatic structure. When you get situations in which the hero, and his friends, and his relatives, and their relatives are star-crossed by destiny, the story becomes far more absorbing, far more personal than any mere tale of the interaction of strangers could ever be. Also, I knew that, given all these factors, the stories would virtually be able to write themselves. And I was right. I've always found that the easiest stories to write are the ones in which the characters are clearly defined and have a close and involved relationship to one another. Then, the writer merely has to think "What if—?" What if Character "A" were to be held hostage, and Character "B" were faced with the problem of yielding to the captors' demands even if it meant thwarting the course of justice? Or, what if Character "C" mistakenly felt that Character "D" had betrayed him? Any of these, or thousands of similar "what ifs," would be sufficient to form the premise of a viable story, provided the characters have enough dramatic integrity and enough appeal to make the reader care about the fate that may befall them.

Well, history has shown (Marvel history, that is) that The Green Goblin certainly had whatever it takes to make the reader care. As for me, I'm delighted to have been able to find the following tale, one which is a landmark adventure in the life of Spider-Man, and which graphically illustrates what I have always considered to be the best, most interesting type of hero/villain relationship—the personal, one-to-one interaction between two human beings in opposition, two protagonists on a collision course along the winding highway of life!

And, with that little venture into melodramatic hyperbole, I'd better clam up and let our sterling little saga speak for itself. Prepare then to leave the workaday world, O Seeker of Truth, and join us for a rollicking romp with the Green Goblin as he launches his most deadly assault upon the amazing Spider-Man, whom he had just captured at the end of the preceding issue! Don't so much as wiggle a web, hear? We're on our way!

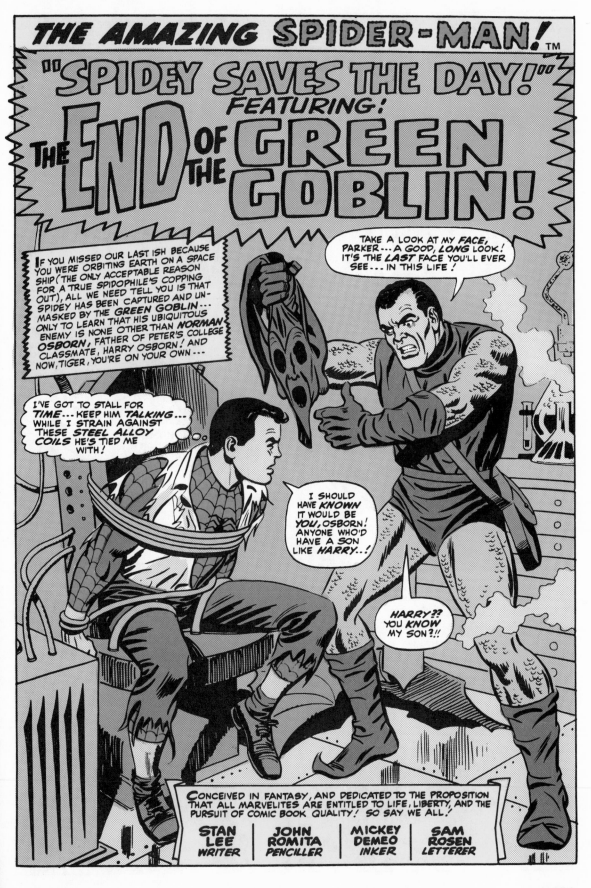

THE AMAZING SPIDER-MAN! ™

"SPIDEY SAVES THE DAY!"
FEATURING!
THE END OF THE GREEN GOBLIN!

IF YOU MISSED OUR LAST ISH BECAUSE YOU WERE ORBITING EARTH ON A SPACE SHIP (THE ONLY ACCEPTABLE REASON FOR A TRUE SPIDOPHILE'S COPPING OUT), ALL WE NEED TELL YOU IS THAT SPIDEY HAS BEEN CAPTURED AND UN-MASKED BY THE GREEN GOBLIN... ONLY TO LEARN THAT HIS UBIQUITOUS ENEMY IS NONE OTHER THAN *NORMAN OSBORN*, FATHER OF PETER'S COLLEGE CLASSMATE, *HARRY OSBORN*! AND NOW, TIGER, YOU'RE ON YOUR OWN...

TAKE A LOOK AT MY *FACE*, PARKER... A GOOD, *LONG* LOOK! IT'S THE *LAST* FACE YOU'LL EVER SEE... IN THIS LIFE!

I'VE GOT TO STALL FOR *TIME*... KEEP HIM *TALKING*... WHILE I STRAIN AGAINST THESE *STEEL ALLOY COILS* HE'S TIED ME WITH!

I SHOULD HAVE *KNOWN* IT WOULD BE *YOU*, OSBORN! ANYONE WHO'D HAVE A SON LIKE *HARRY*...!

HARRY?? YOU *KNOW* MY SON?!!

CONCEIVED IN FANTASY, AND DEDICATED TO THE PROPOSITION THAT ALL MARVELITES ARE ENTITLED TO LIFE, LIBERTY, AND THE PURSUIT OF COMIC BOOK QUALITY! SO SAY WE ALL!

| STAN LEE WRITER | JOHN ROMITA PENCILLER | MICKEY DEMEO INKER | SAM ROSEN LETTERER |

YOU SHOULDN'T HAVE *MENTIONED* HARRY! WHY DID YOU *REMIND* ME OF HIM?

I MUSTN'T *THINK* OF HIM, DO YOU HEAR! I MUST FORGET... *FORGET!*

HE THINKS I'M JUST A SIMPLE *BUSINESSMAN!* HE MUST NEVER KNOW THE TRUTH--- *NEVER!*

AND HE *WON'T!* YOU'LL NEVER TELL HIM! I WON'T *LET* YOU!

THAT'S *ANOTHER* REASON WHY YOU MUST *DIE*, PARKER! ONLY *YOU* KNOW WHO THE GREEN GOBLIN IS!...JUST AS *I* KNOW WHO *SPIDER-MAN* REALLY IS!

BUT WHAT HE *DOESN'T* KNOW IS...I'M JUST AS WORRIED ABOUT *AUNT MAY* LEARNING *MY* SECRET IDENTITY AS *HE* IS ABOUT HARRY LEARNING *HIS!*

I'VE *GOT* TO GET OUT OF THIS SOMEHOW..FOR *HER* SAKE! THE SHOCK WOULD BE MORE THAN SHE COULD BEAR!

I CAN *TELL* THAT YOU'RE STRUGGLING TO BREAK THOSE COILS, PARKER! HOW I *ENJOY* WATCHING YOUR FUTILE, TORTURED EFFORTS!

THAT'S IT, MISTER...STAND THERE AND *GLOAT*...WHILE I KEEP TUGGING AT THESE BLASTED BONDS!

BUT, ENOUGH TALK! NOW I MUST FIND THE MOST *SUITABLE* MANNER OF ENDING YOUR INTERFERENCE FOREVER!

SPIDEY, IF YOU'VE EVER THOUGHT FAST...AND TALKED FASTER....YOU'VE GOTTA DO IT *NOW!*

I THINK THE COILS ARE *LOOSEN-ING!* ALL I NEED IS *TIME!*

GREAT WORK, GOBBY! IT'LL MAKE A REAL *CELEBRITY* OUT OF YOUR SON, HARRY! NOT *EVERY* FELLA CAN HAVE A MURDERER IN THE FAMILY!

I *WARNED* YOU! DON'T *MENTION* HIM!

WHY *NOT?* WHAT HAVE I GOT TO *LOSE?* YOU CAN ONLY POLISH ME OFF *ONCE!*

OSBORN IS OBVIOUSLY A *PSYCHOPATH!* I'VE GOT TO PLAY ON HIS EMOTIONS...GOT TO KEEP HITTING HIM WHERE IT *HURTS!*

ANYWAY, YOU'RE NOT FOOLING *ME!* YOU DON'T GIVE A *HOOT* ABOUT HARRY! HE TOLD ME SO *HIMSELF!* HE TOLD ME HOW YOU'VE *CHANGED* TOWARDS HIM THESE PAST FEW YEARS!

LIES! ALL LIES! HE DOESN'T UNDERSTAND! *NOBODY* UNDER-STANDS! NOBODY REALLY KNOWS *WHY* I BECAME THE GREEN GOBLIN!

I WAS *RIGHT!* HE'S A REAL MENTAL CASE! MY ONLY CHANCE IS TO KEEP *TAUNTING* HIM!

BUT, I'VE GOT TO BE *CAREFUL!* ONE WRONG WORD COULD MAKE HIM *VIOLENT*...AND THEN, BYE-BYE SPIDEY!

BIG DEAL! WHO *CARES* WHY YOU BECAME THE GREEN GOBLIN? YOU PROBABLY LOST AN *ELECTION* BET OR SOMETHING! WHAT DOES IT MATTER?

YOU *FOOL!* I'LL *SHOW* YOU WHAT IT MATTERS! I'LL *MAKE* YOU LISTEN! THEN YOU'LL *UNDERSTAND!*

GOOD! IT'S WORKING!

2.

I HOPE IT'LL BE A LONG STORY! I'VE ONLY MANAGED TO LOOSEN ONE SINGLE FINGER SO FAR! THE WAY HE TIED ME..! I CAN'T EXERT ENOUGH LEVERAGE..!

HARRY'S MOTHER PASSED AWAY WHEN HE WAS JUST A BABY! I HAD TO BRING HIM UP ALONE....AND I TRIED MY BEST..!

SURE, SURE! THEY'LL PROBABLY ELECT YOU FATHER OF THE YEAR... BEFORE THE JUDGE SENDS YOU AWAY!

"I WAS A GOOD FATHER... I WAS! I DID MY BEST TO BE A REAL PAL TO MY SON! BUT, IT WASN'T EASY--!"

YOU'LL HAVE TO HAVE DINNER ALONE TONIGHT, SON! I HAVE TO WORK LATE AGAIN!

THAT'S OKAY, DAD! I UNDER-STAND!

SCHOOL BUS

"AFTER ALL...I HAD A BUSINESS TO TAKE CARE OF! MONEY WAS THE MOST IMPORTANT THING OF ALL! I HAD TO GET RICH! I NEEDED WEALTH..FOR THAT WAS THE KEY TO POWER!"

YOU'LL HAVE TO WORK THESE PROBLEMS OUT YOUR-SELF, HARRY! I'VE GOT TO GET BACK TO THE OFFICE NOW!

BUT YOU SAID YOU'D REVIEW MY BIO WITH ME! I'VE AN EXAM TOMORROW!

YOU'LL JUST HAVE TO DO THE BEST YOU CAN!

"BUT, HARRY DIDN'T HAVE ANYTHING TO COMPLAIN ABOUT! THE MORE MONEY I MADE, THE MORE PRESENTS I BOUGHT HIM! I WANTED EVERYONE TO SEE WHAT A GREAT FATHER HE HAD!"

GO ON, SON... TAKE IT! I JUST BOUGHT IT FOR YOU...AS A SURPRISE!

OH... THANKS, DAD..!

IT'LL GIVE YOU SOMETHING TO DO WHILE I'M OUT OF TOWN ON BUSINESS NEXT MONTH!

"I EVEN TOOK HIM TO BALL GAMES WHEN I HAD A CHANCE! NOBODY CAN SAY I WASN'T A PERFECT FATHER, DO YOU HEAR..? NOBODY!"

DAD, DO YOU THINK... MAYBE WE CAN TALK FOR A WHILE..?

SURE, HARRY, SURE! BUT WATCH THE GAME NOW! WE DON'T WANNA MISS ANY OF THIS!

BUT...WE NEVER HAVE A CHANCE..!

LATER, KID! LATER..!

HE'S SICKER THAN I THOUGHT! HE'S LIVING IN A FANTASY WORLD OF HIS OWN MAKING! HE'S ALMOST FORGOTTEN ME!

BUT, HIS STORY HAS ME HOOKED NOW! I STILL CAN'T FIGURE OUT WHAT MADE HIM BECOME THE GREEN GOBLIN!

HOW COULD I EXPECT HARRY TO UNDERSTAND HOW HARD I HAD TO WORK IN ORDER TO ACHIEVE SUCCESS..?

"I HAD TO BE RUTHLESS IN BUSINESS! I ALLOWED NO ONE TO STAND IN MY WAY...NOT EVEN MY PARTNER... A MAN NAMED PROFESSOR STROMM....!*"

OSBORN! WE'RE PARTNERS! YOU CAN'T DO THIS TO ME!

I WORKED TO BUILD THIS BUSINESS WITH YOU! MOST OF THE INVENTIONS ARE MINE! YOU CAN'T TURN AGAINST ME LIKE THIS!

I ONLY BORROWED THAT MONEY FROM OUR ACCOUNT! YOU KNOW I DIDN'T MEAN TO STEAL IT! IF YOU CALL THE POLICE... I'LL BE RUINED!

IT'S TOO LATE FOR THAT, STROMM! I'VE AL-READY SENT FOR THEM!

*REMEMBER STONY-FACED STROMM FROM SPIDEY #37? SURE YOU DO! ...SMILEY.

3.

163

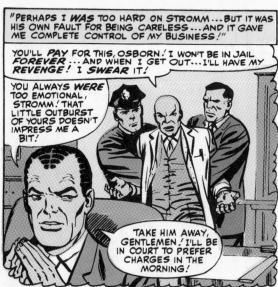

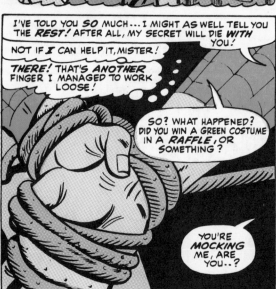
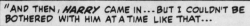

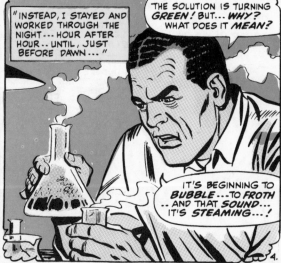

"AND THEN...A SECOND LATER...THE WORLD *EXPLODED* BEFORE ME...!"

WHOOM!

"I WAS IN THE HOSPITAL FOR *WEEKS*, AS THE BEST SURGEONS IN THE STATE WORKED NIGHT AND DAY TO SAVE MY LIFE!"

THE DAMAGE IS DEEP WITHIN HIS *BRAIN!* BUT..THERE'S NO WAY WE CAN *REACH* IT!

AT LEAST WE'VE SAVED HIS *LIFE!* HIS RECOVERY SHOULD BE RAPID NOW!

"THE *FOOLS!* THEY THOUGHT MY BRAIN HAD BEEN *DAMAGED!* THEY DIDN'T SUSPECT THAT THE ACCIDENT MADE ME MORE *BRILLIANT* THAN I HAD EVER *BEEN!* NO ONE SUSPECTED...NOT EVEN MY *SON!*"

YOU MAY SEE YOUR FATHER NOW...

POOR *DAD!* IT'S ALL *MY* FAULT! HE MUST HAVE BEEN OVER-WORKED, TIRED...TRYING TO EARN ENOUGH MONEY TO SUPPORT *ME!*

"BUT, I HAD NO *PATIENCE* WITH HARRY...OR WITH *ANYBODY!* I WANTED TO BE ALONE..TO THINK...TO *PLAN!* SO, A FEW DAYS LATER..."

GO DOWNSTAIRS AND CALL A *TAXI!* I'M GETTING *OUT* OF HERE!

AND GET THAT *HANG-DOG* LOOK OFF YOUR FACE! IT *BOTHERS* ME!

HOW DID SOMEONE LIKE *ME* EVER HAVE A SNIVELLING WEAKLING OF A SON LIKE *YOU*?!!

DAD..WHAT'S *WRONG?* WHY ARE YOU *ANGRY* AT ME? WHA...WHAT HAVE I *DONE*?

YOU HAVEN'T DONE *ANYTHING!* THAT'S THE *TROUBLE!* YOU'RE A SPINELESS JELLYFISH..LIKE EVERY-ONE ELSE!

NOW BE *QUIET!* I'VE GOT TO *CONCENTRATE!*

"ALTHOUGH NOBODY *KNEW* IT, MY ACCIDENT HAD MADE ME THINK *CLEARER* THAN EVER BEFORE! SUDDENLY, A DARING *PLAN* TOOK SHAPE IN MY MIND..!"

I'M STRONGER..SMARTER... *TOUGHER* THAN ANYONE ELSE! AND I HAVE ALL SORTS OF *SCIENTIFIC DEVICES* IN MY CHEMICAL COMPANY THAT I CAN USE!

I COULD BECOME THE GREATEST *COSTUMED CRIMINAL* OF ALL TIME!!

"THE IDEA BECAME AN *OBSESSION* WITH ME! IT HAUNTED ME NIGHT AND DAY! I KNEW I HAD TO *DO* IT! AND SO, MANY MONTHS LATER..."

THE *FACE* IS PERFECT! NOW TO DESIGN THE *REST* OF THE COSTUME!

I'LL MAKE IT MY FAVORITE COLOR... *GREEN!*

5.

"AND SO...AT LAST..THE *GREEN GOBLIN* WAS BORN!"

NOW FOR MY FIRST *VICTIM*...

THE AMAZING *SPIDER-MAN* HIMSELF!

I SELECTED *YOU* BECAUSE I KNEW THE UNDERWORLD WOULD RESPECT ANYONE WHO COULD *DEFEAT* YOU! BUT, YOU *THWARTED* ME DURING OUR FIRST ENCOUNTER!

I'M AWFULLY *SORRY* TO HAVE BEEN SO UNCOOPERATIVE!

I'M STILL *NOWHERE* WITH THESE COILS !! HOW MUCH LONGER CAN I KEEP HIM *TALKING*!

BUT NOW, THE TIME HAS COME FOR THE *GREEN GOBLIN* TO ACHIEVE HIS GREATEST *TRIUMPH*!

I'VE WAITED *MONTHS* FOR THIS SUPREME MOMENT... FOR THIS VICTORY WHICH FATE COULD NEVER *DENY* ME!

I *CAN'T* GIVE UP NOW.. I *MUSTN'T*! FOR THE SAKE OF *AUNT MAY*! BUT.. THE STEEL ALLOY IS TOO *STRONG*...I..I STILL CAN'T *SNAP* IT!.!

HOW *FITTING* IT IS THAT THE FACE OF THE *GREEN GOBLIN* SHALL BE THE *LAST* SIGHT YOU'LL EVER BEHOLD...IN THIS LIFETIME!

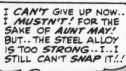

HE WAS JUST A GREEDY, RUTHLESS *BUSINESSMAN* BEFORE HIS ACCIDENT... BUT THE CHEMICAL *CHANGED* HIM ...FOR THE WORSE!

BUT, I MUSTN'T LET THE END BE TOO *EASY* FOR YOU..!

NOW, WHAT DO I *DO* ? HOW DO YOU REASON WITH.. A *MADMAN*?!!

FIRST, YOU MUST *SIT* THERE... HELPLESSLY..AND WONDER *HOW* I SHALL STRIKE... AND AT WHAT PRECISE *INSTANT* YOU'LL PERISH!

6.

THEY SAY A MAN'S *ENTIRE LIFE* FLASHES BEFORE HIM IN A MOMENT OF DEADLY CRISIS! AND, SO IT IS WITH *PETER PARKER* ...

I'M NOT AFRAID TO DIE! I'VE FACED THE GRIM REAPER TOO MANY TIMES IN THE PAST! BUT, NEVER TO SEE *BETTY BRANT* AGAIN... NEVER TO BE ABLE TO EXPLAIN TO *AUNT MAY*...

BEG, PARKER! PLEAD FOR MERCY! WHY WON'T YOU *BEG*??

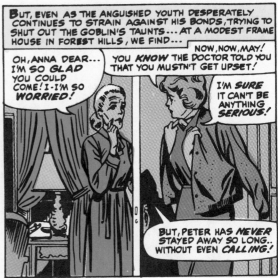

BUT, EVEN AS THE ANGUISHED YOUTH DESPERATELY CONTINUES TO STRAIN AGAINST HIS BONDS, TRYING TO SHUT OUT THE GOBLIN'S TAUNTS ...AT A MODEST FRAME HOUSE IN FOREST HILLS, WE FIND...

OH, ANNA DEAR... I'M SO *GLAD* YOU COULD COME! I-I'M SO *WORRIED*!

NOW, NOW, MAY! YOU *KNOW* THE DOCTOR TOLD YOU THAT YOU MUSTN'T GET UPSET!

I'M *SURE* IT CAN'T BE ANYTHING *SERIOUS*!

BUT, PETER HAS *NEVER* STAYED AWAY SO LONG.. WITHOUT EVEN *CALLING*!

HE'S ALWAYS BEEN SUCH A *GOOD* BOY... BUT HE'S SO FRAIL! I KNOW SOMETHING MUST HAVE *HAPPENED*! I JUST *KNOW* IT!

MAY PARKER! I'M *SURPRISED* AT YOU! YOU GET *HOLD* OF YOURSELF THIS VERY MINUTE!

WHAT WOULD *PETER* SAY IF HE SAW YOU LIKE THIS?

HE'S PROBABLY OUT ON A DATE... HAVING A GOOD TIME... AND HE DOESN'T REALIZE HOW *LATE* IT IS!

EVEN MY *MARY JANE* HAS COME HOME LATE OCCASIONALLY!

BUT... I JUST CAN'T HELP *WORRYING*...!

WAIT A MINUTE! DOESN'T HE SOMETIMES SELL PHOTOGRAPHS TO *MR. JAMESON*, AT THE "DAILY BUGLE"?

PERHAPS HE'S AT JAMESON'S OFFICE RIGHT *NOW*! NEWSPAPER BUILDINGS STAY OPEN ALL NIGHT!

PLEASE, ANNA ... *YOU* CALL! I-I'M TOO *NERVOUS*!

OF COURSE, DEAR! I'LL DO IT RIGHT NOW!

BUT, AFTER FINALLY GETTING PAST AN OVER-WORKED SECRETARY...

NO! PARKER *ISN'T* HERE! WHAT AM *I* SUPPOSED TO BE... A *LOST AND FOUND* DEPARTMENT?!!

HE'S PROBABLY OUT STEALING HUBCAPS SOMEWHERE!

EMPTY-HEADED TEEN-AGERS! THEY'RE ALL *ALIKE*!

MISS BROWN!! COME IN HERE... WITH YOUR *NOTEBOOK*!

I WANT TO DICTATE AN *EDITORIAL* ABOUT HOW THE *YOUNGER* GENERATION'S GOING TO THE *DOGS*!

THEN I'LL DO ONE ABOUT THE *OLDER* GENERATION, TOO!

MIGHT AS WELL *BLAST* EVERY-ONE!

SLAM!

AND, AFTER MRS. WATSON HAS GIVEN MAY PARKER THE NEWS...AS GENTLY AS POSSIBLE...

YOU *MUSTN'T* WORRY, DEAR! THERE ARE SO MANY *OTHER* PLACES HE MIGHT BE!

ANNA..YOU DON'T *KNOW* PETER THE WAY *I* DO!

HE'S THE MOST *CONSIDERATE* BOY IN THE WORLD!

HE'D *NEVER* STAY OUT LATE WITHOUT *CALLING* ME!

..UNLESS.. *SOMETHING'S HAPPENED*...!

HE MIGHT BE IN *TROUBLE* SOMEWHERE! HE MIGHT *NEED* ME! IF ONLY I *KNEW!*

OH, PETER... PETER...

I'M GOING *OUT* FOR A MOMENT, MAY... BUT I'LL BE RIGHT *BACK,* HEAR? YOU JUST WAIT RIGHT THERE, DEAR... AND TRY NOT TO WORRY!

SHE'S GETTING *OVERWROUGHT!* SHE NEEDS A *SEDATIVE!* I'VE GOT TO CALL DR. BROMWELL!

MEANWHILE, AT A RAILROAD STATION IN THE MIDWEST, ANOTHER FEMALE WHO HAS PLAYED AN IMPORTANT ROLE IN THE LIFE OF PETER PARKER PAUSES BETWEEN TRAINS..

I *MUST* RETURN TO NEW YORK! I REALIZE NOW THAT A GIRL CAN NEVER RUN FROM A DECISION..

NO MATTER *HOW* PAINFUL IT MAY BE!

THIS IS *ART ROBERTS,* AT STATION *WLS* IN CHICAGO, WONDERING WHY NOTHING HAS BEEN HEARD OF *SPIDER-MAN* THESE PAST FEW DAYS...

SPIDER-MAN!! THE MASKED ADVENTURER WHOM PETER ADMIRES! HOW I HATE THE VERY SOUND OF HIS NAME!

HE REPRESENTS EVERYTHING I DREAD... *DANGER... UNCERTAINTY...* AND *FEAR!*

BUT, WHY DWELL ON SPIDER-MAN WHEN I HAVE A FAR *BIGGER* PROBLEM !?

IF I RETURN TO THE *DAILY BUGLE,* WILL MR. JAMESON GIVE ME MY OLD JOB BACK?

AND, IF HE DOES.. WHAT WILL IT BE LIKE, SEEING *PETER PARKER* AND *NED LEEDS* AGAIN?

AND, WHAT WILL THEY SAY WHEN THEY SEE *ME?* WILL THERE STILL BE A PLACE IN THEIR LIVES FOR... *BETTY BRANT?*

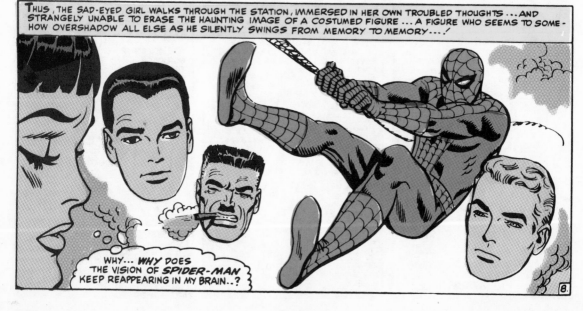

THUS, THE SAD-EYED GIRL WALKS THROUGH THE STATION, IMMERSED IN HER OWN TROUBLED THOUGHTS ... AND STRANGELY UNABLE TO ERASE THE HAUNTING IMAGE OF A COSTUMED FIGURE ... A FIGURE WHO SEEMS TO SOMEHOW OVERSHADOW ALL ELSE AS HE SILENTLY SWINGS FROM MEMORY TO MEMORY...!

WHY... *WHY* DOES THE VISION OF *SPIDER-MAN* KEEP REAPPEARING IN MY BRAIN..?

8.

168

WHEN I THINK OF ALL THE TIMES I'VE *SEEN* SPIDER-MAN...SPOKEN TO HIM...AND YET, HE'S AN *ENIGMA!*

HE COULD BE *ANYBODY...* EVEN SOMEONE WHOM I *KNOW!*

BUT..I HOPE..AND *PRAY...* THAT HE *ISN'T!* I COULDN'T *STAND* IT IF HE WERE SOMEONE CLOSE TO ME...SOMEONE WHOM.. I *LOVE!*

ALL ABOARRRD!

PERHAPS, WHEN I RETURN TO NEW YORK...AND SEE *PETER* AGAIN...I'LL BE ABLE TO *FORGET* ABOUT SPIDER-MAN... FOREVER!

AS YOU PROBABLY GUESSED BY NOW, THE PAGES YOU'VE JUST READ ARE A TYPICAL MARVEL DEVICE FOR BRINGING NEW READERS UP TO DATE AS PAINLESSLY AS POSSIBLE! (WE JUST DIDN'T WANT YOU TO THINK YOU'D PICKED UP A ROMANCE BOOK BY MISTAKE!) BUT NOW, *FACE FRONT!* IT'LL BE *WEB-SPINNIN'* TIME BEFORE YOU KNOW IT..!'

SO! YOU THINK YOU CAN ROB ME OF MY *SATISFACTION* BY SITTING THERE WITH YOUR EYES CLOSED!

WELL, IT WON'T *WORK!!*

THAT'S *IT,* GOBLIN! RANT AND RAVE AT ME...SAY *ANYTHING*... JUST SO LONG AS YOU KEEP *TALKING!*

NO! YOU *LIE..* DO YOU *HEAR??* YOU LIE! YOU *NEVER* BEAT ME!!

IF ONLY I CAN KEEP *GOADING* HIM!

YOU'RE A *WASHOUT,* MAN! I BEAT YOU EVERY TIME WE FOUGHT BEFORE----AND I'LL FIND A WAY TO BEAT YOU *AGAIN!*

I'LL *PROVE* IT TO YOU!

I CAN PROJECT *MENTAL PICTURES* OF OUR PREVIOUS BATTLES BY MEANS OF THIS *RETRO-SCOPE* HELMET!

I'LL *SHOW* YOU THAT YOU NEVER BEAT ME! I WAS *ALWAYS* YOUR *MASTER!!* ALWAYS!

SURE! SURE! *ANYTHING* TO GIVE ME MORE *TIME!*

THERE! I'M SURE YOU REMEMBER *THOSE* THREE!

THE *ENFORCERS!* IT WAS THE FIRST TIME WE FOUGHT...YOU USED THEM TO *HELP* YOU!*

CLICK!

* SPIDEY # 14, NATCH!...STAN.

9.

BUT, HOW DOES *THIS* PROVE ANYTHING? I WAS ABLE TO LICK THEM *ALL! THERE...* YOU CAN *SEE* IT!

BUT YOU DIDN'T *BEAT ME!*

THAT BATTLE TAUGHT ME A *LESSON!* IT TAUGHT ME THAT *NO ONE* CAN DO MY FIGHTING FOR ME! *NO ONE* IS AS GREAT AS THE *GREEN GOBLIN!*

THAT SO? JUST CUT THESE *STEEL COILS* FROM MY WRISTS, AND IT'LL BE THE GOBLIN'S *LAST GOBBLE!*

NEVER! YOU *HAD* YOUR CHANCE... AND YOU *MUFFED* IT!

THEN, THE NEXT TIME WE FOUGHT, YOU WERE *SAVED* BY THE SUDDEN APPEARANCE OF THE *HUMAN TORCH...!*

BUT I HAD NO DESIRE TO FIGHT *HIM!* IT WAS *YOU* WHO WERE THE ENEMY!

*SPIDEY #17... AS IF YOU DIDN'T KNOW! ...S.

THEREFORE, I *FLED...* ALLOWING YOU TO *ESCAPE* ME! BUT, *YOU* DIDN'T BEAT ME.. INSTEAD YOU WERE SIMPLY SAVED BY THE *TORCH!*

THAT'S *YOUR* VERSION, GOBLIN! FROM WHERE *I* SAT, YOU RAN LIKE A SCARED RABBIT!

YOU'LL *PAY* FOR THAT REMARK, PARKER!

BUT, ONCE AGAIN I MADE THE MISTAKE OF ALLYING MYSELF WITH OTHERS! SO IT WAS THAT *LUCKY LOBO* AND HIS GANG WERE MORE OF A *HINDRANCE* THAN A HELP WHEN NEXT WE MET!*

*IF YOU DON'T BELIEVE US, CHECK BACK TO *SPIDEY* #23! WE KID YOU NOT! ...S.L.

NOT ONLY DID YOU FAIL TO *STOP* ME, BUT YOU WERE LUCKY THAT I LET YOU ESCAPE WITH YOUR *LIFE!*

A *PITY,* SPIDER-MAN, THAT YOU WILL NOT HAVE THAT SAME LUCK *THIS* TIME!

AND NOW, THE *FINAL* REMEMBRANCE... BEFORE YOU MEET YOUR *END!*

DURING OUR MOST *RECENT* BATTLE, I HAD YOU COMPLETELY *BEATEN!* EVEN *YOU* CANNOT DENY THAT!

BUT, ONCE *AGAIN*, YOU WERE SAVED BY A STROKE OF FATE... IN THE GUISE OF THE *CRIME-MASTER!**

* ALL TOGETHER NOW, CLASS: *"SPIDEY #27!"* SCHOLARLY STAN.

" THINKING HE WAS A MATCH FOR THE *GREEN GOBLIN*, THE MASKED FOOL DARED TO ATTACK ME... ONCE AGAIN GIVING *YOU* A CHANCE TO ESCAPE!"

"YOU NEVER *WERE* ANY GOOD AS A *FIGHTER*, SPIDER-MAN!! YOU WERE MERELY *LUCKY!*"

" BUT, AS I FLEW OFF TO SAFETY, ON THAT FATEFUL DAY... ALLOWING YOU A FEW MONTHS MORE OF *LIFE*, I KNEW I WOULD AGAIN RETURN... WHEN YOU LEAST EXPECTED ME... TO *FINISH* THE TASK I HAD SET FOR MYSELF.. NAMELY.."

".. THE COMPLETE AND UN- DENIABLE *DESTRUCTION* OF THE AMAZING *SPIDER-MAN!*"

IT *WORKED!* I KEPT HIM TALKING LONG ENOUGH TO FREE *ONE HAND!* NOW, IT'LL JUST BE A MATTER OF *SECONDS* TO RIP THE *OTHER* COILS AWAY...!

SO! YOU'RE STILL STRUGGLING WITH YOUR BONDS, ARE YOU? I CAN TELL BY THE WAY YOUR *MUSCLES* ARE TENSED BENEATH YOUR SHIRT!

WELL, I'LL MAKE IT *EASY* FOR YOU... SINCE YOU'RE ALREADY *DOOMED!*

IT WOULD HAVE BEEN AN *EMPTY VICTORY* TO DEFEAT A FOE WHO IS HELPLESSLY SHACKLED!

THEREFORE, I'LL *SET YOU FREE!* I'LL *PROVE* I'M YOUR MASTER!

YOUR FINAL THOUGHT... BEFORE THE *END* COMES... WILL BE THAT I GAVE YOU EVERY CHANCE... AND *STILL* I DEFEATED YOU.. UTTERLY AND *ETERNALLY!*

YOU FAST-TALKING *PHONY!* YOU *KNEW* I WAS ABOUT TO BREAK LOOSE *ANYWAY!* *THAT'S* WHY THE GRAND- STAND PLAY!

OKAY, PARKER! THIS MAY BE THE MOST FATEFUL FIGHT OF YOUR *LIFE!* SO DON'T FUMBLE THE BALL, FELLA... THERE'S TOO MUCH AT *STAKE!*

RRAKK!

11.

172

HAVE YOU SO SOON *FORGOTTEN* THE PEERLESS *POWERS* WHICH THE GREEN GOBLIN POSSESSES?

BA-KOOO!

SURE! JUST AS I'D FORGOTTEN WHAT A FULL-TIME, ECONOMY-SIZE *CORNBALL* YOU REALLY ARE!

SO! THE CONDEMNED MAN HELD ON TO HIS SLENDER FACADE OF WANING COURAGE TILL THE VERY *END*, EH?

MY *COMPLIMENTS*, SPIDER-MAN! TOO BAD YOUR *POWER* IS NOT EQUAL TO YOUR COURAGE!

HE'S HOPPING ON HIS JET-POWERED *GOBLIN GLIDER!* NOW HE'LL BE *TRICKIER*.. MORE *MANEUVERABLE* THAN EVER!

LET ME CAUTION YOU AGAINST TRYING TO SNEAK UP *BEHIND* ME...

..UNLESS YOU *ENJOY* THE FULL BRUNT OF A *ROCKET BLAST!*

WHROOSH!

HE'S *TOYING* WITH ME! HE FEELS SO *CONFIDENT*, THAT HE'S WARNING ME IN ADVANCE!

I'VE NEVER BEEN *FACED* WITH A PROBLEM LIKE THIS BEFORE! EVEN *DEFEATING* HIM WON'T HELP ME...

FOR, SO LONG AS HE *LIVES*, HE KNOWS MY *SECRET IDENTITY!* AND, IF AUNT *MAY* EVER LEARNS OF IT.. I *LOSE*... EVEN THOUGH I MAY HAVE *WON!*

SSSSSS

HAH! YOU'RE *GROGGY*.. *CONFUSED*..!

...AS I KNEW YOU *WOULD* BE!

SO, NOW I FINISH YOU OFF, AND... *UNHHH!*

WOK!

THANKS, *GOBBY!* I *HOPED* YOU'D COME WITHIN REACH IF I ACTED HELPLESS ENOUGH!

13.

173

174

175

178

SECONDS LATER...

OH, *NO!* IT.. IT'S WHAT I *FEARED!*

THAT'S *DR. BROMWELL'S* CAR AT THE DOOR!

BUT.. I'VE GOT TO BE *CAREFUL!* CAN'T LET ANYONE SEE ME LIKE *THIS!*

I'VE GOT TO GET TO MY ROOM THROUGH THE BACK WINDOW--- AND *CHANGE* UP THERE!

POOR AUNT MAY! IF... IF ANYTHING *HAPPENS*.. I'LL NEVER *FORGIVE* MYSELF!

IT WILL BE BECAUSE SHE WAS *WORRIED* ABOUT *ME!*

WHY MUST I *HURT* EVERYTHING I TOUCH?? UNCLE BEN! BETTY BRANT! AND NOW---AUNT MAY!

BETTY'S FEMALE *INTUITION* MUST HAVE MADE HER LEAVE ME!

SHE MUST HAVE *FELT* THAT I'D BRING NOTHING BUT *HEARTACHE* TO THOSE I LOVE!

THE *AMAZING SPIDER-MAN!* ABLE TO CLIMB WALLS....TO *FIGHT,* TO *RUN,* TO *THINK* BETTER AND FASTER THAN ANY DOZEN ORDINARY MEN!

EVEN THOSE WHO *HATE* ME ENVY MY POWERS!

MY *POWERS!* WHAT A *JOKE!*

I SOMETIMES THINK THEY'VE PROVEN TO BE NOTHING BUT A *CURSE!*

I-I'D TRADE PLACES WITH ALMOST *ANY* NORMAL EVERYDAY MAN!

AT LEAST *AUNT MAY* WOULDN'T HAVE TO SUFFER FOR MY SECRET!

DR. BROMWELL! MY *AUNT!* IS SHE..??

QUIET, SON! SHE FINALLY FELL *ASLEEP!* I'VE PLACED HER UNDER MILD SEDATION!

IT WASN'T *EASY* TO GET HER TO SHUT HER EYES! SHE WAS VERY *CONCERNED* ABOUT YOU, PETER!

I-I WAS *AFRAID* OF THAT, DOCTOR!

YOU *WERE?*

THEN WHY DID YOU STAY OUT SO LATE WITHOUT *CALLING?* I *WARNED* YOU THAT SHE MUST BE SPARED FROM ANY SERIOUS WORRY, OR SHOCK!

I NEVER THOUGHT THAT *YOU'D* BE SO *UNFEELING* ...SO WRAPPED UP ONLY IN *YOURSELF!*

AND THERE
SHALL COME A MONSTER!

It happened in the early part of 1967. I was talking with some of the guys in the Bullpen. Just to prove how much I trust you, I'll let you listen in.

"You're crazy," they said.

"Why?" I cleverly replied.

"Because" was the devious, well-considered answer. They thought they had me stumped with that one, but I came right back at them.

"Because why?" See? I've always thought quickly on my feet.

"Because the Abomination is a lousy name for a villain!" That one really hurt. Especially since I was the guy who had thought up the name.

As you've probably surmised by now, the gang and I were discussing a new villain to be used in our latest *Hulk* spectacular. I had everything all worked out to my total satisfaction. The entire plot was clear as crystal in my mind and I couldn't wait to start typing the script itself. Then I happened to mention the name I had chosen for my newest little super wrongdoer, and that's when everything hit the fan.

Many times have I said there's no place in the hallowed halls of Marvel for a sycophantic yes-man. We want people who think for themselves—creative geniuses who have the courage of their own convictions, free and independent souls who bow to no man's will. Many times have I said it. Ever have I meant it. Always do I seek it. And yet, every so often I get the feeling that it might not be so bad to have someone agree with me right from the start—just once! Of course, I wouldn't have it any way but the way it is. And yet. And yet . . .

But, getting back to that fateful day in question: there I was, my back figuratively against the wall, besieged on all sides by well-meaning Bullpenners, attempting to save me from myself, to protect me from the folly of the name I had chosen for our latest supervillain. "None of our younger readers will know how to pronounce it!" "Abomination! What kinda name is that, fer Pete's sake?" "Half our readers won't even know what it means!" "And the other half'll think we're puttin' them on!" And so it went.

Well, in the immortal words of Richard Milhous, "When the going gets tough, the tough get going!" The more they protested, the more determined I was to stick with The Abomination! I had had it up to here with names like The Purple Potato or The Living Bedspread. And we'd just about exhausted the animal kingdom, what with The Ox, The Lizard, The Scorpion, The Vulture, and possibly The Awesome Amoeba waiting in the wings. And then, of course, we had no shortage of "Man" titles, either. There was The Mole Man, The Absorbing Man, The Titanium Man . . . but why go on? You get the idea. I felt a name like The Abomination was needed; not necessarily because it was good—just 'cause it would be different!

The rest is history. I managed to convince everyone to go along with my title through sheer logic and canny reasoning ability—coupled with the fact that I was the editor. So the die was cast. The Abomination he would be. 'Twas a fateful day indeed for the fabled world of legend!

And now that I've proven how much space can be wasted on something that could just as easily be described in a few sentences, let's go on to the meat of the matter. What was the underlying philosophy behind the creation of The Abomination? Gosh, I'm glad you asked.

We had, as you know, great success with The Incredible Hulk. In a few short years he seemed to have become everybody's favorite Jolly Green Giant. But he had, and still has, one built-in problem that's always been tough to lick. He's so incalculably powerful that we drive ourselves bananas trying to find villains capable of giving him a good enough battle. I mean, you can't exactly see a green-skinned rampager who weighs over a ton and can wreck the Brooklyn Bridge with his bare hands battling Aunt May, can you? And yet, once he's confronted someone like The Mighty Thor eyeball-to-eyeball, and a few other superguys who might be in that league, who's left? Well, that's what started me thinking.

It seemed to me that it would be a kick to have The Hulk in combat with some sort of foe who'd have the same power as he did. In fact, the more I thought about it, the more the notion grabbed me. One of the most distinctive things about ol' Hulky is the color of his skin. It's a sure bet that there aren't too many guys in your local gym or delicatessen whose epidermis matches their bright green socks from their toes to the tops of their flat little heads. Not only would I come up with an opponent who'd match The Hulk power for power, but I'd even give him the same color skin. I liked it. I liked it.

Now came the tough part. How would The Abomination get that way? From whence cometh his super power? What would ever make him the equal of The Hulk? It came to me in a flash as soon as I decided to give him green skin also. It was a gamma ray accident that gave The Hulk his power—and his green skin. Okay. All I had to do was invent another gamma ray accident and I'd accomplish both objectives at once—the power *and* the skin. That was it. Although I really shouldn't reveal how simple it is. Next thing we know everyone will be going out and inventing Hulks, Abominations, and Heaven knows what else!

Along about now, Garrulous Gil Kane had been drawing the *Hulk* strip for quite a while—which figures, since he's dazzlingly drawn practically every strip we have at some time or other, as most of Marvel's greatest artists had done during those elysian early days. Thus, the fantastically facile and fabulous Gil was faced with the task of designing a monstrous being who would resemble The Hulk while still being totally different. It's a tribute to G.K.'s aplomb that he didn't even bat an eye, lose his cool, or stop talking for a minute. Of course, Gil has never been known to stop talking for any period of time, but that's another matter. Picking up his trusty pencil he applied himself to his fateful task, and before you could say "Dr. Bruce Banner stole a banana," the job was done. The Abomination was born. The Hulk had a new enemy to battle. I had a new character's name to learn to remember—and to spell—a name that would become part of our mighty Marvel heritage, and which would make the world a better place to live in—each time The Hulk put the whammy on 'im!

Incidentally, you might remember the time The Thing was created, in the premiere issue of *The Fantastic Four*. Do you recall how Jack Kirby drew him with only four fingers and toes? It used to drive everyone crazy trying to remember that it was The Thing who had four fingers and The Hulk who had five. I can't tell you how many times other artists and inkers would get confused and put the wrong number of fingers and/or toes on one or both of our two melancholy monsters. Well, leave it to good ol' Gil to make matters even worse. Before we knew it, he had drawn The Abomination with the requisite amount of fingers, but—with only two toes! Pretty soon we'll have to give our proofreaders combat pay if we want them to hang around.

Anyway, we did call him The Abomination, and he did prove to be another Marvel headliner. And this time, for a change, I don't even have to apologize for the mixed-up sequence of stories. This time we actually showed his origin in the very first two tales in which he appeared. No complications. No voluminous footnotes required. Everything straightforward and simple. There's no doubt about it—someone must have goofed!

One final thought. If you have trouble remembering the name Abomination, don't worry about it. I'll give you a foolproof way to brand it into your brain. Just bear in mind that it sort of rhymes with transmogrification. See? Now you'll never forget it. And now it's time to turn the page and see how whatever-his-name-is really got started. . . .

GRIMLY WATCHING THE ENTIRE TITANIC TABLEAU IS THE ONE *RESPONSIBLE* FOR THE HULK'S RAMPAGE...THE UNEARTHLY, SUPREMELY-POWERFUL *STRANGER*--!

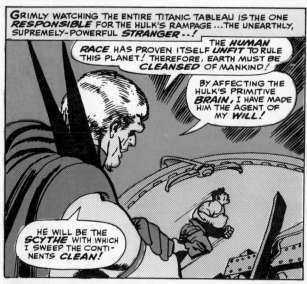

THE *HUMAN RACE* HAS PROVEN ITSELF *UNFIT* TO RULE THIS PLANET! THEREFORE, EARTH MUST BE *CLEANSED* OF MANKIND!

BY AFFECTING THE HULK'S PRIMITIVE *BRAIN*, I HAVE MADE HIM THE AGENT OF MY *WILL!*

HE WILL BE THE *SCYTHE* WITH WHICH I SWEEP THE CONTINENTS *CLEAN!*

NOW, *OTHER* MATTERS IN FAR-DISTANT GALAXIES REQUIRE MY PRESENCE!

BUT, WHEN I *RETURN*, THE HULK'S *STRENGTH* SHALL HAVE SERVED ME WELL!

BY DESTROYING VITAL INSTALLATIONS WHEREVER HE FINDS THEM, HE WILL HAVE *SOFTENED* HUMANITY UP... FOR THE KILL!

BUT, ALTHOUGH UNABLE TO THINK OR REASON FOR HIMSELF, SOME HALF-BURIED *INSTINCT* LEADS THE GREEN TITAN TOWARDS A DISTANT MISSILE BASE...

THOOM!

MUST SMASH EVERYTHING I *SEE*...EVERYWHERE!!

MUST DESTROY WEAPONS... SO PUNY MEN CAN'T FIGHT *BACK!*

THEN, IN A SERIES OF THE MOST MONUMENTAL, DISTANCE-DEVOURING *LEAPS* EVER RECORDED, HE REACHES HIS DESTINATION AT *LAST*...MOVING TOO FAST...TOO LOW...TO BE DETECTED BY THE EARLY-WARNING *RADAR*--!

MIGHTIEST WEAPONS OF *ALL* DOWN BELOW!!

MUST *FIND* THEM!! MUST WRECK MOST *POWERFUL* ONES FIRST!

BUT... WHICH IS... *WHICH?*

WITHOUT WARNING, THE SUDDEN STRAIN OF TRYING TO *THINK* CAUSES AN UNEXPECTED REACTION...

MY *HEAD*... SPINNING! GETTING *WEAK!* STARTING TO *FALL!*

SOMETHING *HAPPENING* TO HULK!! BUT... *WHAT*...??

SECONDS LATER, AS HIS BODY GROWS *SMALLER*, THE CLOUDED BRAIN BEGINS TO *CLEAR*--- UNTIL...

I'M TURNING INTO *BRUCE BANNER* ONCE MORE!

MUST LAND... QUICKLY...WHILE I STILL RETAIN *SOME* OF THE HULK'S STRENGTH---TO CUSHION THE SKY-HIGH *FALL!*

MY HEAD IS *CLEAR* NOW! I REMEMBER *EVERYTHING!*

THE *STRANGER* TOOK CONTROL OF THE *HULK'S* BRAIN---BUT, NOW THAT I'M *BRUCE BANNER* ONCE MORE, HIS POWER OVER ME HAS *VANISHED!*

AND THEN, THE ONE THING WHICH EVEN THE *STRANGER* HADN'T ANTICIPATED, OCCURS...

THE WORLD IS *SAFE* FROM THE SHATTERING ONSLAUGHT OF MY OTHER SELF!

OR....*IS* IT SAFE ??!

2

I CAN'T REMAIN BRUCE BANNER *FOREVER*! SOONER OR LATER I'LL CHANGE BACK TO THE *HULK* AGAIN... AS I'VE DONE SO OFTEN IN THE *PAST*!

AND, WHEN I *DO*... WHAT IF I MUST *OBEY* THE STRANGER'S *DEADLY COMMAND* ONCE MORE?

WHAT IF *NOTHING* CAN STOP ME *NEXT* TIME?

I CANNOT... I *DARE* NOT TAKE THE AWESOME *CHANCE*!

ONLY *ONE* THING WILL INSURE THE SAFETY OF MANKIND...

THE HULK MUST DIE!

EVEN THOUGH IT MEANS THE DEATH OF *BRUCE BANNER*, AS WELL!

RIGHT *HERE*,. ON THIS POST...IS THE POTENT *GAMMA RAY MACHINE* WHICH I MYSELF CREATED!

I'VE GOT TO *REACH* IT BEFORE I BECOME *TRANSFORMED* AGAIN!

ONE SINGLE *OVERDOSE* OF ITS FATAL RAYS, AND THE MENACE OF THE *HULK* WILL BE ENDED....*FOREVER*!

MEANWHILE, AT ANOTHER PART OF THE BASE, GENERAL *THUNDERBOLT ROSS* HAS CALLED AN URGENT MEETING OF HIS TOP SECURITY OFFICERS ---

GENTLEMEN, AN ATTEMPT ON THE LIFE OF MY DAUGHTER, *BETTY*, HAS BEEN MADE BY AN UNIDENTIFIED ASSAILANT!

THREE SEPARATE ATTEMPTS TO *SABOTAGE* OUR MOST VITAL MISSILES HAVE BEEN NARROWLY NIPPED IN THE BUD!

WE *KNOW* THERE'S A *FOREIGN AGENT* OPERATING HERE ON THE POST--BUT HE'S MANAGED TO SLIP THROUGH OUR FINGERS TIME AND AGAIN!

WE'LL *GET* HIM, GENERAL! HE CAN'T EVADE US MUCH LONGER! IT'S JUST A MATTER OF *TIME*!

DID YOU *HEAR* THAT, GENTLEMEN? *MAJOR TALBOT* TELLS US IT'S JUST A MATTER OF *TIME*!

WELL, I'VE SOMETHING TO TELL THE *MAJOR*.. AND *ALL* OF YOU...!!

WE'VE PLUMB RUN *OUT* OF TIME!

I WANT THAT BLASTED *SPY CAUGHT*... AND I WANT HIM CAUGHT *NOW*!!

THE SECURITY OF THIS ENTIRE *MISSILE COMMAND*--- OF THIS ENTIRE *NATION*---MAY BE AT STAKE!

IF I DON'T GET *RESULTS*, I'LL TAKE IT OUT OF YOUR *HIDES*!! I'LL *BREAK* EVERY *ONE* OF YOU..!!

DO I MAKE MYSELF *CLEAR*??!

NOW *GET GOING*!! YOU HAVE YOUR ORDERS! *OBEY* THEM!! *BRING ME THAT SPY*!!

HE'S CLEVER--AND HE'S *DANGEROUS*!! TAKE NO *CHANCES*!! WHEN YOU'VE *NAILED* HIM, SHOOT TO *KILL*, IF NECESSARY!

WE'LL *GET* 'IM, GENERAL! YOU CAN *COUNT* ON IT!

BETTY! WHAT *IS* IT? WHAT'S *WRONG*?

OH, GLEN... I'M *FRIGHTENED*! *BRUCE* HAS BEEN MISSING--FOR DAYS!!

WHAT IF *HE*... OR THAT HORRIBLE *HULK*---ARE MIXED UP IN ANY OF THIS??

HAVE I *FOUND* HIM--AFTER ALL THAT'S HAPPENED--- ONLY TO *LOSE* HIM ONCE MORE---*FOREVER*?

WOULDN'T IT BE *BETTER* IF YOU *DID* LOSE HIM? ALL HE'S EVER *DONE* IS... BREAK YOUR HEART!

3.

AT THAT MOMENT, IN THE NOW-DESERTED LAB OF *DR. BRUCE BANNER,* A MERCILESS, STEELY-EYED INTRUDER, IN THE STOLEN UNIFORM OF A POST *M.P.,* THINKS HIS OWN DARK THOUGHTS...

IF I HAD SUCCEEDED IN CAPTURING THE GENERAL'S *DAUGHTER,* MY TASK MIGHT HAVE BEEN *SIMPLER!*

I COULD HAVE HELD HER *HOSTAGE* FOR MY OWN SAFETY!

BUT, I CAN AFFORD TO WAIT *NO LONGER!*

I *MUST* GET PICTURES OF THE *GAMMA RAY MACHINE*---NO MATTER *WHAT* THE COST!

THERE ARE THOSE BEHIND THE BAMBOO CURTAIN WHO WILL PAY *ANY PRICE* FOR BANNER'S INVENTION!

IF ANYONE *FINDS* ME HERE, I'LL CLAIM I WAS SEARCHING FOR THE ENEMY *SPY* WHOM EVERYONE IS SEEKING!

WHAT SUPREME *IRONY*...TO USE MY OWN *PRESENCE* AS MY OWN *DEFENSE!*

ANOTHER FEW PICTURES WITH MY SPECIAL *SUB-MINIATURE CAMERA,* AND THE JOB WILL BE *DONE!*

CLICK!

CLICK!

FOOTSTEPS!! SOMEONE'S COMING!

I *CAN'T* BE INTERRUPTED *NOW*... I'M NOT YET *FINISHED!*

I'LL FIND A PLACE TO *HIDE*...AND WAIT TILL HE *LEAVES!*

THUP!

THUD!

I'M IN *LUCK!* MY LAB'S *EMPTY!*

IT'S BANNER *HIMSELF!* WHAT CAN HE *WANT* HERE NOW?

I CAN'T *HESITATE*-- CAN'T PUT IT OFF FOR A SINGLE *MINUTE!*

IT MUST BE *DONE* BEFORE I CAN CHANGE INTO THE *HULK* AGAIN!

CLASK!

THERE! THE *SAFETY* IS OFF! NOW IT'S JUST A MATTER OF *TIME!*

BUT, BEFORE THE SELF-SACRIFICING SCIENTIST CAN PROPERLY *POSITION* HIMSELF IN FRONT OF THE FATE-FUL *GAMMA RAY*--

HOLD IT, BANNER!! WE'VE BEEN LOOKING HIGH AND LOW FOR YOU!

GRAB HIM, MEN... BEFORE HE CAN UTILIZE THAT *MACHINE!*

THE M.P.'S!!

WAIT!! STOP! YOU DON'T *UNDERSTAND!* I *MUST* BE LEFT ALONE WITH THESE *GAMMA RAYS!*

SO YOU CAN CHANGE BACK TO THE *HULK* AND GET *AWAY* FROM US? IT WON'T *WORK,* BANNER!

NO! LISTEN TO ME! LET ME *EXPLAIN*--!

IT'S FOR *YOUR* SAKE...FOR THE SAKE OF *HUMANITY!* DON'T STOP ME *NOW*--!

WE HAVE OUR *ORDERS,* MISTER! YOU'RE WASTING YOUR BREATH!

4.

AND, AS THE VAINLY-PROTESTING PRISONER IS DRAGGED AWAY...

WHATEVER HE WAS *UP TO,* THEY NIPPED HIS PLAN RIGHT IN THE BUD!

BUT, HE SURE DID *WANT* TO GET IN FRONT OF THAT *MACHINE* OF HIS!

I WONDER *WHY?*

BANNER'S THE *GREATEST* ATOMIC SCIENTIST OF THEM ALL! WHATEVER HE WAS *AFTER*---IT MUST HAVE BEEN SOMETHING REALLY *BIG!*

AND NOW... *I'VE* GOT THE CHANCE TO *FIND OUT!*

THIS COULD BE THE *GREATEST* THING I'VE EVER STUMBLED ONTO!

THIS IS WHERE *BANNER* WANTED TO STAND! NOW, LET'S SEE...

THAT *FOOT CONTROL* MUST ACTIVATE THE APPARATUS!

PTHIPP!

AND THEN, THE INCREDIBLE OCCURS ONCE MORE!!

WHAT...WHAT'S *HAPPENING* TO ME??

---I'M *CHANGING!!*

IT..MUST BE... THE SAME PROCESS... THAT CHANGED *BANNER*... INTO THE *HULK*...!

I'VE GOT TO... *STOP* IT!! I DIDN'T *KNOW*... DIDN'T *SUSPECT*...!!

BUT, BEFORE ANOTHER MOVE CAN BE MADE...BEFORE ANOTHER WORD CAN BE UTTERED--THE DREADED *GAMMA RAYS* HAVE DONE THEIR FRIGHTFUL WORK---!

TOO LATE TO STOP!! HAH!! DON'T *WANT* TO STOP!! I'M *DIFFERENT*... MORE *POWERFUL!!*

I'M STRONG AS THE *HULK!!* I CAN DO *ANYTHING!!* I'M MASTER OF THE *WORLD*--- OF THE WHOLE *UNIVERSE!!*

191

NO ONE CAN STAND UP TO ME!! NO ONE CAN STOP ME! I AM INVINCIBLE!

AND THEN, WITHOUT REALIZING IT, THE NEWLY-CREATED MONSTROUS BEING UN-WITTINGLY SAVES HIS OWN LIFE...!

I'LL SMASH THE MACHINE... SO THAT NO ONE ELSE CAN EVER BE AS POWER-FUL AS I!!

--FOR, HAD HE BEEN BOMBARDED BY THE INDESCRIBABLY POTENT RAYS JUST A FEW SECONDS LONGER, THE FORMER SPY WOULD HAVE SUFFERED THE SAME FATE WHICH BRUCE BANNER HAD INTENDED FOR THE HULK..

THUBOOM!

HAH!! NOW, THERE ARE ONLY TWO OF US... ME.. AND THE BRAINLESS GREEN HULK!

BUT, SOON ONLY ONE WILL REMAIN!!

FOR, ONCE I DESTROY HIM... MY STRENGTH WILL BE THE GREATEST! MY POWER WILL BE SUPREME!

NOW, ALL THAT REMAINS TO DO IS... FIND HIM!

BTAM!

AND, FIND HIM I WILL..!!

THERE'S ROOM FOR ONLY ONE LIVING, GREEN-SKINNED POWERHOUSE HERE ON EARTH..*

AND THAT ONE IS ME!!

*AS WE HAVE SEEN, THE MYSTERIOUS GAMMA RAYS AFFECT EVERYONE THEY TOUCH IN A DIFFERENT MANNER! MANY MONTHS AGO, THEY GAVE THE NOW-DEAD LEADER THE MOST BRILLIANT MIND ON EARTH! WHEN THEY TRANSFORMED BRUCE BANNER INTO THE HULK, THEY SUBSTITUTED POWER FOR INTELLIGENCE! AND NOW..THEY HAVE CREATED THE ABOMINATION YOU SEE BEFORE YOU!

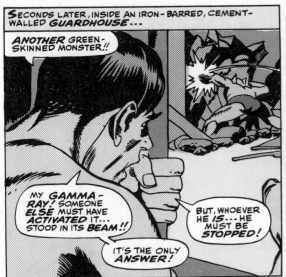

SECONDS LATER, INSIDE AN IRON-BARRED, CEMENT-WALLED *GUARDHOUSE*...

ANOTHER GREEN-SKINNED MONSTER!!

MY *GAMMA-RAY!* SOMEONE ELSE MUST HAVE *ACTIVATED* IT... STOOD IN ITS *BEAM!!*

IT'S THE ONLY *ANSWER!*

BUT, WHOEVER HE *IS*---HE MUST BE *STOPPED!*

THEN, IN HIS EXCITEMENT...THE *TENSION* WITHIN BANNER'S BRAIN AGAIN TRIGGERS HIS AWESOME *TRANSFORMATION*--

AND, HE CAN *ONLY* BE STOPPED BY...

THE *HULK!*

SKRUNTCH!

CRRAK!

NO ONE KEEPS HULK IN CELL!

ALTHOUGH HIS NOW-CLOUDED BRAIN HAS ALREADY *FORGOTTEN* HIS REASON FOR ATTACKING THE *ABOMINATION* ---ONCE STARTED, THE *HULK* CAN NEVER *STOP* HIS BESTIAL CHARGE--!

THE *HULK!!*

~OOMP!

THOOMP!

FINALLY, AS THE DEAFENING *IMPACT* SEEMS TO SHAKE THE SURROUNDING *MOUNTAINS* THEMSELVES, THE TWO GREAT, GAMMA-POWERED *GOLIATHS* CLASH IN MORTAL COMBAT...

HULK WILL STOP YOU!!

THIS IS YOUR *FINISH*, YOU GRUESOME GARGOYLE!!

EVEN IF YOUR OWN *STRENGTH* CAN MATCH *MINE*...I'VE THE *BRAINS* TO THINK.. TO *OUT-PLAN* YOU!!

WHRUOOM

7.

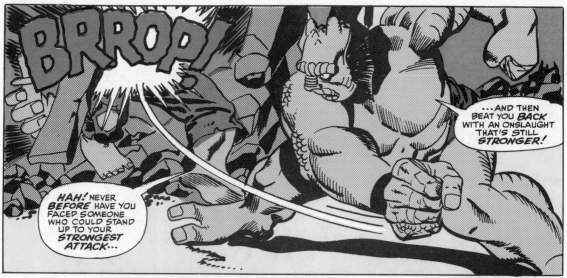

BRROP!

...AND THEN BEAT YOU *BACK* WITH AN ONSLAUGHT THAT'S STILL *STRONGER!*

HAH! NEVER *BEFORE* HAVE YOU FACED SOMEONE WHO COULD STAND UP TO YOUR *STRONGEST ATTACK*...

NO ONE BEATS HULK BACK... *NO ONE!!*

BRAINLESS BEAST!! YOU HAVEN'T THE SENSE TO REALIZE ...YOU'RE *DOOMED!!*

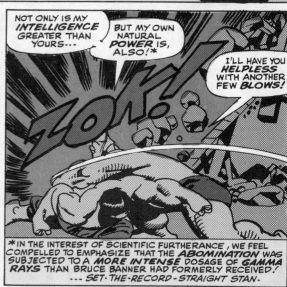

NOT ONLY IS MY *INTELLIGENCE* GREATER THAN *YOURS*...

BUT MY OWN NATURAL *POWER* IS, *ALSO!**

I'LL HAVE YOU *HELPLESS* WITH ANOTHER FEW *BLOWS!*

ZOK!

*IN THE INTEREST OF SCIENTIFIC FURTHERANCE, WE FEEL COMPELLED TO EMPHASIZE THAT THE *ABOMINATION* WAS SUBJECTED TO A *MORE INTENSE* DOSAGE OF *GAMMA RAYS* THAN BRUCE BANNER HAD FORMERLY RECEIVED! ---SET-THE-RECORD-STRAIGHT STAN.

DAD! WHO.. OR *WHAT*.. CAN THAT *ABOMINATION* BE?

I DON'T *KNOW*, BETTY... BUT YOU'VE CHOSEN A PERFECT *NAME* FOR IT!!

HE'S BEATING BACK THE *HULK!!* IF.. IF HE ISN'T *STOPPED*.. HE'LL *KILL* HIM! HE'LL *KILL* BRUCE BANNER!

IF ONLY THEY'D FINISH OFF *EACH OTHER!* PERHAPS, IF THEY KEEP *FIGHTING*..!

NO..!

THE *HULK* HASN'T A *CHANCE!*

THE *OTHER* ONE IS TOO *POWERFUL!* LOOK... THERE'S NO *STOPPING* HIM!

THEY CALLED ME AN *ABOMINATION*--- AND THEY'RE *RIGHT!*

BAM!

WHEN *I'M* THROUGH MENACING MANKIND, THEY'LL WISH THEY HAD *ONLY* THE *HULK* TO WORRY ABOUT!

BUT, BY THEN, *YOU'LL* BE NO MORE THAN A FORGOTTEN *MEMORY!*

8.

AND NOW... I'M THROUGH *TOYING* WITH YOU!!

NOTHING THAT *LIVES* CAN SURVIVE A BLOW LIKE *THIS*--!

NOT EVEN... THE *HULK!*

KRAK

IT'S *ENDED!!* NOW, THE *ABOMINATION* IS THE MOST POWERFUL LIVING MORTAL ON THE FACE OF THE EARTH!!

NO *LONGER* NEED I RESORT TO BEING A FURTIVE *SPY*...!

NOW, I HAVE ONLY TO DESIRE A GOAL... AND I POSSESS THE *STRENGTH* TO MAKE IT *MINE!*

9.

BUT, *OTHERS* HAVE BEEN WATCHING!!

SO LONG AS I *REMAIN* HERE, I AM VULNERABLE TO ATTACK BY THEIR *MISSILES* AND *ROCKETS*!!

AND, I HAVEN'T YET *LEARNED* WHETHER OR NOT I CAN *SURVIVE* SUCH AN ATTACK!

THE *ABOMINATION* IS TOO *CLEVER* TO CARELESSLY RISK HIS NEW-FOUND POWER *NOW*!

HENCE, I SHALL TAKE MY *LEAVE*... TEMPORARILY!!

AND, TO INSURE *NO PURSUIT*, I'LL TAKE A *HOSTAGE* WITH ME!

NO! NO!! LET ME GO...!!

STOP HIM! HE *CAN'T*... HE *MUSTN'T*... UHHH!

STOP ME?? YOU *PUNY* FOOLS...

...STOP ME... **HOW?!!**

EVERYTHING THE *HULK* COULD DO.... I CAN DO.. AND *BETTER*!!

BETTY!! HE'S GOT MY *DAUGHTER*!!

HE'S LEAPING *AWAY* WITH HER.... AND WE *DARE NOT* FIRE AFTER THEM... FOR FEAR OF *HITTING* HER!

WE'LL *GET* HIM, SIR! SOMEHOW.. SOME WAY.. WE'LL *GET* HIM!!

BUT... HE'S *POWER PERSONIFIED*... WITH A NORMAL *INTELLIGENCE*, TO BOOT!!

HE'S THE *GREATEST LIVING THREAT* EVER TO FACE US...EVER TO MENACE THE NATION...OR, THE *WORLD*!!

BUT, HE MUST HAVE A *WEAKNESS*.... AND, IF HE *DOES*, WE'LL *FIND* IT!! WE'VE *GOT* TO FIND IT!

THERE'S ONLY *ONE* BEING WHO MIGHT HAVE CAUGHT HIM.... WHO MIGHT HAVE *STOPPED* HIM..!

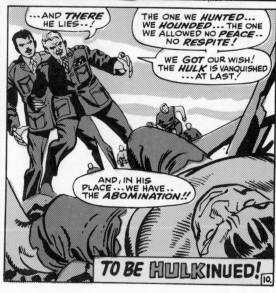

...AND *THERE* HE LIES..!

THE ONE WE *HUNTED*... WE *HOUNDED*... THE ONE WE ALLOWED NO *PEACE*.. NO *RESPITE*!

WE GOT OUR WISH! THE *HULK* IS VANQUISHED ...AT LAST!

AND, IN HIS *PLACE*.. WE HAVE.. THE *ABOMINATION*!!

TO BE HULKINUED! 10.

LOOK AT HIM--THE ROTTEN, BRAINLESS, RAMPAGING MADMAN!

ALL HIS STRENGTH--HIS BESTIAL POWER--MEANT NOTHING WHEN IT COUNTED THE MOST! THE ABOMINATION MADE MINCE-MEAT OUT OF HIM!

BUT, HE TRIED, GENERAL! WE'VE GOT TO GIVE HIM THAT! HE DID THE BEST HE COULD!

IF ONLY HE WERE STILL ALIVE! HE MIGHT YET BE ABLE TO LEAD US TO BETTY!

OUR OWN JETS ARE TOO FAST! THE ABOMINATION COULD EASILY HIDE FROM THEM! BUT, THE HULK--!

OF COURSE!! WHY DIDN'T WE THINK OF THAT, INSTEAD OF WASTING TIME?!

GENERAL! LISTEN! HOW DO WE KNOW HE'S DEAD?? WHAT IF--?

SERGEANT!! GET THOSE MEN OVER HERE--ON THE DOUBLE!

LIFT HIM OFF THE GROUND--EASY, EASY WITH HIM, BLAST IT!

NOW, GET HIM TO BANNER'S LAB!

I'LL GET THE MEDIC, SIR! I'LL HAVE HIM WAITING AT THE LAB BY THE TIME THEY REACH IT!

IF THERE'S ANY CHANCE OF REVIVING HIM-- WE'LL DO IT!!

AWRIGHT, YOU HEARD THE GENERAL! LET'S GO!!

HIS BODY'S STILL WARM, SARGE! MAYBE HE IS STILL ALIVE!

M.P.

THE ABOMINATION HAS DISAPPEARED OVER THE HILLS WITH BETTY! HE COULD BE HIDDEN ANY-WHERE BY NOW!

THE HULK HAS TO BE ALIVE-- HE HAS TO!!

HE'S THE ONLY ONE WHO HAS A CHANCE OF GOING AFTER THEM--OF MATCHING THAT MONSTER'S GIGANTIC LEAPS!

HE MUSTN'T DIE! THE HULK MUSTN'T DIE!

MOMENTS LATER, IN BANNER'S LAB, A GRIM-FACED SURGEON TENSELY SCRUTINIZES THE MOTIONLESS GREEN GIANT...

THERE'S STILL A PULSE--BUT IT'S WEAK--AND GETTING WEAKER!

IT'S A MIRACLE THAT HE'S ALIVE AT ALL!

HE TOOK ENOUGH PUNISHMENT TO HAVE DESTROYED A HUNDRED MEN!

HIS BODY IS SO STRANGE--SO INCREDIBLY DIFFERENT--IT DOESN'T RESPOND TO NORMAL TREATMENT!

I'M AFRAID --IT'S HOPELESS!

2

MEANWHILE, IN THE CORRIDOR OUTSIDE--

YOU CAN'T KEEP ME OUT! THE HULK'S HURT--HE NEEDS ME! I'VE GOTTA SEE HIM!

COME BACK HERE, KID! THAT LAB'S OFF-LIMITS!

IT'S RICK JONES--THE HULK'S ONLY FRIEND!

HEY, YOU GUYS-- STOP 'IM!

I DON'T CARE IF IT'S GUNGA DIN!! WE'VE GOT OUR ORDERS!

THOP! THUD! THUMP!

WHAT'SA MATTER WITH YA? HE'S ONLY ONE KID!

YEAH-- BUT HE'S SLIPPERY AS AN EEL, AND YOU DON'T EXPECT US TO SHOOT 'IM?!!

IT'S OKAY! HE'LL NEVER GET THRU THE DOOR WHILE I'M HERE!

GENERAL! GENERAL ROSS! ARE YOU IN THERE? IT'S ME--RICK JONES! LEMME IN-- YOU'VE GOTTA LET ME SEE THE HULK!

GRAB 'IM! HE'S REALLY POPPED HIS CORK NOW!

BUT, A SPLIT-SECOND LATER--

OPEN THAT DOOR! LET THE BOY IN!

BUT, GENERAL-- YOUR ORDERS WERE--!

HANG MY ORDERS!! MAYBE JONES KNOWS SOMETHING THAT WE DON'T!

WITH THE ABOMINATION RUNNING LOOSE, WE'RE NOT PASSING UP ANY CHANCE!

THE GAMMA ELECTRODES! IF ANYTHING'LL REVIVE HIM, THEY WILL! BUT YOU GOTTA HURRY--!

THUS, AS THE TENSION GROWS THICK ENOUGH TO BE FELT BY ALL--

GENERAL, IF THIS DOESN'T WORK, I REQUEST PERMISSION TO LEAD A PLATOON OF VOLUNTEERS INTO THE HILL--!

IT WOULD TAKE YOU DAYS TO REACH 'EM, TALBOT! THE HULK COULD DO IT IN MINUTES!

QUIET, GENTLEMEN! THIS IS IT!

I'VE SET THE GAMMA ELECTRODES AT FULL STRENGTH!

THERE'S NOTHING MORE WE CAN DO-- EXCEPT PRAY!

THTAK

K!K!

ZZZ

NOTHING'S HAPPENING! IT ISN'T WORKING!! IT--

WAIT! LOOK! HE STIRRED--!

3

"SET RANGE O-X23-ZY! MOVE, MAN! WE'RE NOT PLAYING GAMES HERE NOW!"

"DOC--WHAT'LL YOU DO-- WHEN HE GETS HERE?"

"YOU'LL SEE WHEN THE TIME COMES!"

"PUT TWO MEN AT THAT VIDEO SCANNER! STEP ON IT!"

"REPORT ANYTHING YOU SEE!"

"DR. BANNER!! IT'S THE ABOMINATION! HE'S HEADING THIS WAY! --IT'S AS THOUGH SOME-THING'S DRAWING HIM TO THE SPOT!!"

"SOMETHING IS PULLING HIM HERE! IT'S THE DOC'S INFINITE GAMMA RAY! IT HAS TO BE!"

"LOOK AT THOSE MUSCLES RIPPLE--LOOK AT HIS SPEED --HIS POWER!!"

"HOW WILL WE EVER BE ABLE TO HANDLE HIM??"

"AS SOON AS HE GETS CLOSER-- CLEAR OUT--THAT MEANS ALL OF YOU!"

"IT'S GOT TO BE MY SHOW FROM HERE ON IN!"

"I DON'T GET IT!"

"IF HE'S STRONGER THAN THE HULK-- HOW CAN ANYTHING STOP 'IM?"

SECONDS LATER, AS THE REMAINDER OF THE PERSONNEL HASTILY EVACUATE THE AREA--

"SOMETHING KEPT PULLING ME HERE-- LIKE A TORMENTING MAGNET THAT I CAN'T RESIST!"

"WHATEVER IT IS, IT'S COMING FROM THE LAB--JUST AHEAD--!"

"THE CLOSER I GET, THE STRONGER THE PULL!"

THROOOM!

BTAM!

"BANNER!! THEN--IT'S YOUR DOING!! IT'S THAT RAY YOU'RE OPERATING!"

"HE'S PUTTING HER DOWN! GOOD! IT'S WHAT I WANTED!"

"THE GIRL WILL BE SAFE ENOUGH-- WHILE I FINISH YOU OFF FOREVER!"

"AND NOW --WHILE HE'S RIGHT IN POSITION --!"

KLIK!

"ARGHH!"

"NO! NO! YOU CAN'T-- YOU CAN'T!!"

"EACH SECOND IN FRONT OF THE RAY WILL SAP YOUR STRENGTH --!"

"JUST ANOTHER FEW MINUTES,' IF ONLY THE BEAM WILL HOLD HIM THERE--!"

NOOO!

BUT, EVEN THE PLAN OF THE BRILLIANT BRUCE BANNER CAN GO ASTRAY--AS WE ARE ABOUT TO SEE IN THE NEXT SPLIT-SECOND---

205

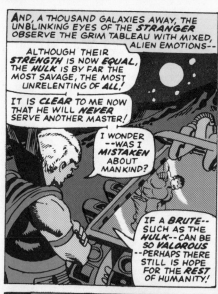

AND, A THOUSAND GALAXIES AWAY, THE UNBLINKING EYES OF THE *STRANGER* OBSERVE THE GRIM TABLEAU WITH MIXED, ALIEN EMOTIONS--

ALTHOUGH THEIR *STRENGTH* IS NOW *EQUAL*, THE *HULK* IS BY FAR THE MOST SAVAGE, THE MOST UNRELENTING OF *ALL!*

IT IS *CLEAR* TO ME NOW THAT HE WILL *NEVER* SERVE ANOTHER MASTER!

I WONDER --WAS I *MISTAKEN* ABOUT MANKIND?

IF A *BRUTE*-- SUCH AS THE *HULK*--CAN BE SO *VALOROUS* --PERHAPS THERE STILL IS HOPE FOR THE *REST* OF HUMANITY!

BUT, HE WHO IS CALLED THE *ABOMINATION* IS TRULY *EVIL!*

THAT, COUPLED WITH HIS HULKISH *POWER*, SHOULD MAKE *HIM* THE HIRELING I SEEK!

THUS, I SHALL BRING HIM *TO* ME--FOR, HE WILL NOT BE *MISSED* UPON THE EARTH!

MANKIND-- *FAREWELL!* THE *STRANGER* HAS OTHER INTERESTS--IN OTHER WORLDS!

AS THE *ABOMINATION* HURTLES TO MY SIDE, I *LEAVE* YOU--AS I *FOUND* YOU--FREE TO SEEK YOUR OWN DESTINY!

AND, I NOW *REMOVE* ANY SEMBLANCE OF MY *CONTROL* WHICH MIGHT STILL REMAIN WITHIN THE MIGHTY *HULK!*

MY *HEAD!*-- LIKE SOME- THING *SNAPPED* --INSIDE MY BRAIN--!

HULK!! YOU'VE *DONE* IT! YOU *WON!* THE *ABOMINATION* IS--*GONE!*

HE SAVED MY *DAUGHTER*--AND DEFEATED THE WORST MENACE TO CONFRONT US!

BUT, SO LONG AS HE STILL REMAINS THE *HULK*-- *WHAT ARE WE TO DO* WITH HIM??!

STAY BACK!! DON'T WANT PEOPLE AROUND ME--!

HULK MUST BE *FREE!* HULK MUST *GO*--!

AND, WHERE THE *HULK* WALKS-- --HE WALKS-- *ALONE!*

NEXT

THE NEW CHAPTER!

10

206

PART
7

MEPHISTO™

BLAZE OF FIRE!
SCENT OF BRIMSTONE!

I'd like to quit right now. I just took a second look at the title of this chapter, and I'm stunned. It's living poetry! It's probably the best title I've ever come up with. Can't you just see it on the next Bob Dylan album? What's the point of writing any more? Anything else from here on in will just be second best. However, we've got a few more pages to fill—and I'm game if you are.

Actually, it's kind of tough for me to kid around with anything that has to do with The Silver Surfer. I really take this character and his stories seriously. In fact, some readers have told me I take them too seriously. They're practically the only stories I've ever written that I haven't attempted to gag up somewhere or other. I just can't do it. It would be like trying to poke fun at a T.V. Telethon's poster girl. The Surfer has such a mystical quality, such quasi-religious implications, that making light of him or his stories would be tantamount to scribbling graffiti on the Sistine Chapel. I even *think* about him in capital letters. So, when it came time to create the ultimate villain for Norrin Radd to battle, I had many a sleepless night before I finally came up with—Mephisto!

Frankly, he was the only possible choice. The Silver Surfer is an allegorical representation of all that is good, all that is pure and unsullied in the human condition. To me, he represents humanity, not as it is but as it might be, as it should be, as it one day must be. His total selflessness and his loathing of violence, greed, and deceit seem to place him on a par with the greatest heroes in the annals of religious legend. A man such as this, with power such as his, must inevitably be confronted by the most universally recognized symbol of evil on the face of the earth—the specter of Satan.

However, I didn't want to hit the reader over the head with religious implications. Basically, it has always been my desire to have our stories savored for their enjoyment value primarily. Any moralistic or philosophical extras which might be thrown in are merely Marvel bonuses. Hence, I was reluctant to use the name Satan, or Mephistopheles, or Lucifer, or whatever. Names such as those would leave nothing in doubt. So I settled for a name which certainly had the sound of Mephistopheles, but we weren't quite coming out and saying it. Besides, Mephisto is easier to spell.

At this point, I have to pause and put in a word or two for Big John Buscema. To say he's one of the greatest artists in comics is like saying the Pacific is a large body of water. To say he's an artists' artist would still be putting it too mildly. When you see the power, the passion, and the pure pulsating pageantry of the artwork that awaits you, you'll realize why I find myself at a loss for words. Certainly few strips have been as favored as The Silver Surfer. To have been originally designed and illustrated by Jack Kirby, and then to have had an entire series drawn with the magic of John Buscema—no wonder the gleaming sky-rider of the spaceways enjoys one of the largest cult followings of all.

Of course, we did have one tremendous problem. How does someone—even a cosmic-powered herald of the great Galactus—engage in battle with Satan himself? How could the Surfer hope to survive the lethal attack of the Ruler of the Stygian Deep? It's easy enough to ask these questions—but I had to find the answers.

Working in collaboration, John and I spent far more time refining each plot, discussing each incident, planning each encounter than we had ever done on any of the dozens of other strips we had worked on in the past. Something about The Silver Surfer seems to affect everyone connected with the series; you get a feeling that everything must be perfect—that nothing must go wrong.

One of the more knotty problems is the matter of language. I always seem to come up with characters that get me into a bind. Here we have the Surfer himself, a brooding creature from far beyond the stars. Now we can hardly have him talk like a typical Joe College. He can't use slang, he'd be a stranger to street talk, and yet the readers might find him insufferably dull if he were merely to speak in simple, uncolorful, declarative sentences. So I had him sound off in my own version of a semi-poetic, pseudo-Biblical, quasi-classical style. If it doesn't quite come off, no wonder. It's tough enough for me to even understand what I just said, let alone to do it!

210

Yet the hardest part was still to come. I had written enough Silver Surfer scripts previously to feel somewhat secure in the style I was attempting. But then came Mephisto. How could I give him essentially the same type of speech patterns, and still make him sound different from our hero? For nothing is as dull, as much of an aural turn-off, as reading the dialogue of two different people whose speech is more or less identical. I soon found myself spending half an hour on a dialogue balloon for Mephisto which I could have written in five minutes or less if it were intended for The Sandman or Doctor Octopus. Even the things I didn't write seemed to take forever. I have a hunch I'd better explain that last remark. You see, in a strip like the *Silver Surfer,* with artwork like Buscema's, I'd have to think long and hard before adding one unnecessary caption or dialogue balloon, because any copy at all would have to replace a corresponding amount of illustration. In other words, the less I'd write the more of Big John's drawings you would see. So, each time I penned a single word, I'd cry a little, inwardly.

I must admit that there is one thing about Mephisto that made it a bit easier to employ him in a script. The fact that he is such a total and complete entity of evil, so unregenerately villainous, with not a single, solitary redeeming quality is a point in his favor. It makes it easy for the writer to understand him, to predict his moves and reactions. For, never forget, even though these characters are the products of a writer's brain, the minute you start to pen the story, they attain a life of their own, a will of their own, a seeming compulsion of their own—and any writer worth his salt must think of them as living, breathing people, must get to know them, to learn how they tick, how they feel, what makes them do the things they do. The better you know your characters, the easier it is to plot their actions and to handle their dialogue. In my own case, I become so much a part of each story I write that my wife frequently comes into the room to ask me if I'm talking to anybody. Unconsciously, I'll mouth the words which I'm writing for each character, and if they don't sound right as I'm saying them, if they don't actually ring true to my own ear, I discard the dialogue and start all over again. I suspect a psychiatrist would have a field day if he were to hide in my room when I'm writing dialogue for a Mephisto, or a Silver Surfer, or even a Shalla Bal! (She's the gal the Surfer has to rescue, and how he does it took all my ingenuity and used up at least a dozen of John's best pencils.)

One last thing I feel compelled to mention, and then we'll savor "The Power and the Prize" together. Remember me telling you how I hate to think of my dialogue obscuring any of J.B.'s magnificent pencilling? Well, in case you've ever wondered why the dialogue balloons in my stories seem to go all over the place, the top of the panels, the bottom of the panels, the sides of the panels, even between the panels and underneath the panels, that's the reason. I always indicate the placement of the captions and balloons myself, and sometimes I'd spend more time deciding where the copy should go than I spent actually writing it. Now that I've let you in on one of our most closely guarded secrets, perhaps it will increase your enjoyment of the story to know the reason that certain copy has been placed in certain areas. But, if you'd rather ignore the whole thing and just concentrate on the yarn itself, go ahead. I'm famous for my deep compassion.

And so the time has come to meet Mephisto as he leaves the sanctuary of his netherworld kingdom in order to slay the Silver Surfer. The Master of Evil won't appear till page seven of the story, but we don't think you'll be too impatient. There are a few things going on that just might hold your interest. Let's not waste another minute. The battle of the ages is about to begin.

BUT, EVEN AS NAMELESS *FEAR* AND MOUNTING *PANIC* SPREAD O'ER THE EARTH LIKE SOME FOUL AND FATAL *FUNGUS*, WE TURN OUR ATTENTION *ELSEWHERE*--TO A WORLD *BEYOND* THE FARTHEST BORDER OF IMAGINATION--YET, *CLOSER* THAN THE NEAREST *NIGHTMARE*--!

IF WE *LISTEN*--WITH RAPT ATTENTION--WE SHALL HEAR A *VOICE*-- LIKE NONE YOUR HUMAN *EAR* HAS EVER HEARD-- LIKE NONE THE HUMAN *MIND* CAN E'ER CONCEIVE--!

PREPARE THE *MYSTIC VAPORS*-- FOR I WOULD *BEHOLD* WHAT NOW OCCURS UPON THE PLANET OF *HUMANS*!

SO SPEAKS MEPHISTO!

ALL IS *READY*, LORD OF *EVIL*!

THAT WHICH *MEPHISTO* COMMANDS SHALL EVER COME TO *PASS*!

FOR, SUCH IS THE *WAY*-- AND SUCH IS THE *POWER* OF HIM WHO RULES THE *STYGIAN DEEP*!

7

220

THEN, AS THE MYSTIC *VAPORS* BRING FORTH THEIR FLICKERING IMAGERIES--

THERE! *THAT* IS WHAT I SEEK!

A BROODING *FIGURE*-- STEEPED IN *PAIN!*

A MOUNTING *PANIC* ENGULFS THE PLANET!

MORE VAPORS!! I MUST NOW LEARN THE *CAUSE!*

HOW OFT *BEFORE* HAVE I TREMBLED IN THE PRESENCE OF SUCH AWESOME *GOODNESS*...

MARTYRS ALL, WHOM MEN THEM-SELVES--IN THEIR ABYSMAL MADNESS--DID FORSAKE!

AS THE MASTER *COMMANDS--!*

AND NOW, HE *TOO* HAS BEEN *FORSAKEN*--HE *TOO* HAS BEEN *DENIED!*

9.

221

222

LOOK! THE FOG--IS LIFTING!

THE CITY IS RETURNING TO NORMAL!

IT'S LIKE SOME KINDA BAD DREAM--THAT SUDDENLY ENDED!

AND, IN HEAVILY-GUARDED DEFENSE ESTABLISHMENTS THRUOUT THE WORLD--

CONDITION BLUE! THE EMERGENCY IS LIFTED!

RE-SECURE ALL MISSILES!

NO ADMITTANCE

WHEW! I THOUGHT THIS WAS FINALLY THE BIG ONE--FOR SURE!

BUT THEN, SUDDENLY--UNEXPECTEDLY--

SIR!! U.F.O. APPROACHING THIS SECTOR!

--IGNORING ALL REQUESTS FOR IDENTIFICATION!

THEN WHAT HAPPENED BEFORE WAS JUST A PRELUDE--TO A NEW ATTACK!

I HAVE UNDONE ALL THAT--WAIT!

A SPACECRAFT--FROM THE PLANET ZENN-LA--MY OWN HOME WORLD!

IT CANNOT BE!!

AND YET--IT IS! IT IS!

14

230

SINCE THE *DAWN OF TIME*-- SELDOM HAVE I SENSED SUCH *GOODNESS OF SOUL*-- SUCH *PURITY OF SPIRIT*-- AS I SENSE WITHIN THE *SILVER SURFER!*

ALL THAT YOU *ARE*-- ALL THAT YOU *STAND FOR*--IS ABHORRENT TO THE LORD OF THE LOWER DEPTHS!

SO LONG AS YOU *EXIST*, MEPHISTO'S *SCHEME SUPREME* WILL EVER BE IN JEOPARDY!

BUT, YOUR *DEMISE* MUST BE AT A PLACE OF *MY* CHOOSING-- UNDER CONDITIONS *I* SELECT!

AND, WITH HIM-- *SHALLA BAL!*

THEREFORE, THE SILVER SURFER MUST *DIE!*

HE IS *VANISHED!*

20

234

"TO ONE SUCH AS I-- IT WAS *CHILD'S PLAY* TO FOLLOW A TRAIL OF-- *BRIMSTONE!!*"

"AND, THOUGH IT HAS BROUGHT ME TO THE MOST *DIABOLICAL* DOMAIN IN ALL THE WORLD--"

"I'D BRAVE A *THOUSAND* TIMES A *THOUSAND* SUCH PLACES OF THE DAMNED--FOR THE LIFE OF *SHALLA BAL!*"

I HAVE FAR *MORE* CAUSE TO DESPISE YOU THAN I *THOUGHT!*

YOUR VERY *GOODNESS* FILLS ME WITH A *LOATHING* TOO GREAT TO *ENDURE!*

WHY DO YOU NOT *CRINGE* WHEN I *APPROACH* YOU??

YOU CAN DO NO MORE THAN *SLAY* ME!

AND *DEATH* HOLDS NO TERROR FOR THE *SILVER SURFER!*

BUT IT *SHALL!* BEFORE THIS STARK CHARADE IS ENDED-- OH, HOW IT *SHALL!*

NOW, *FOLLOW* ME--THAT YOU MAY LEARN--YOUR *FATE!*

24

236

240

242

244

EPILOGUE

And so it ends—for now.

In our own fearless fashion, we've attempted to usher you behind the scenes of our little dream factory for a guided tour through the early days of Marvel Comics. Within the pages of our brave little Origins trilogy we've traced the birth and the growth of some of our greatest heroes and villains.

Now, looking back at these memory-filled pages, I find there's so much more I could have, and perhaps should have said. And the chances are, someday I will. But, for now, let these valiant volumes stand as an enduring monument to the artists and writers who have made Marvel Comics such a vital force in the creation of our modern mythology.

Until we meet again, then, let's hope we shall always carry a love for legend and laughter within our hearts. For, if man should lose his heroes, he surely would lose a bit of his soul as well.

Excelsior!